PRESTWICK HOUSE

Activity Pack

MYTHOLOGY: TIMELESS TALES OF GODS AND HEROES

BY EDITH HAMILTON

ISBN-10   1-58049-608-3
ISBN-13 978-1-58049-609-7

Reorder No. 200119

Mythology: Timeless Tales of Gods and Heroes

Table of Contents

Mythology: Timeless Tales of Gods and Heroes

Activity Pack
Teacher's Edition

Note: All references come from the Warner Books Edition of *Mythology: Timeless Tales of Gods and Heroes*, by Edith Hamilton, copyright 1969.

Pre-Reading

Objective: Researching the historical periods of ancient Greece.

Activity I

The first evidence of real settlement in Greece comes from about 55,000 B.C.E. At that time, there was only a small population, which did not grow until around 3,000 B.C.E. The development of Greek civilization is divided into three main periods—Stone Age, Bronze Age, and Iron Age—and each of these periods can be broken down into subdivisions.

Put together a class newspaper about the history of Greece. In your group, assign individuals to cover the topics of politics, literature, religion, art and architecture, and social development. Gather information on your topic via the Internet and any other reference material available. Feel free to gather any pictures that may enhance the quality of your work. The group will then combine information to create an article for its assignment and save it. When all the groups have composed an article, the class will combine efforts to create a paper.

Mythology: Timeless Tales of Gods and Heroes

Activity Pack
Student Edition

Note: All references come from the Warner Books Edition of *Mythology: Timeless Tales of Gods and Heroes*, by Edith Hamilton, copyright 1969.

Pre-Reading

Objective: Researching the historical periods of ancient Greece.

Activity I

The first evidence of real settlement in Greece comes from about 55,000 B.C.E. At that time, there was only a small population, which did not grow until around 3,000 B.C.E. The development of Greek civilization is divided into three main periods—Stone Age, Bronze Age, and Iron Age—and each of these periods can be broken down into subdivisions.

Put together a class newspaper about the history of Greece. In your group, assign individuals to cover the topics of politics, literature, religion, art and architecture, and social development. Gather information on your topic via the Internet and any other reference material available. Feel free to gather any pictures that may enhance the quality of your work. The group will then combine information to create an article for its assignment and save it. When all the groups have composed an article, the class will combine efforts to create a paper.

Pre-Reading

Objective: Appreciating the moral and political views of ancient Greece.

Activity I

Read the excerpt and answer the questions that follow:

Pericles' funeral oration

As political and military leader of Athens, 460-429 B.C.E., Pericles delivered this eulogy at a mass funeral of troops who had died of plague in the early years of the Peloponnesian War. It is reported to be one of the great proclamations of the civic, aesthetic, moral, and personal virtues of the Athenian city-state.

"Our system of government does not copy the institutions of our neighbors. It is more the case of our being a model to others, than of our imitating anyone else. Our constitution is called a democracy because power is in the hands not of a minority but of the whole people. When it is a question of settling private disputes, everyone is equal before the law; when it is a question of putting one person before another in positions of public responsibility, what counts is not membership of a particular class, but the actual ability which the man possesses. No one, so long as he has it in him to be of service to the state, is kept in political obscurity because of poverty....

We [obey] those whom we put in positions of authority, and we obey the laws themselves, especially those which are for the protection of the oppressed, and those unwritten laws which it is an acknowledged shame to break....

When our work is over, we are in a position to enjoy all kinds of recreation for our spirits...all the good things from all over the world flow in to us, so that to us it seems just as natural to enjoy foreign goods as our own local products....

Our love of what is beautiful does not lead to extravagance; our love of the things of the mind does not make us soft. We regard wealth as something to be properly used, rather than as something to boast about. As for poverty, no one need be ashamed to admit it: the real shame is in not taking practical measures to escape from it. Here each individual is interested not only in his own affairs but in the affairs of the state as well: even those who are mostly occupied with their own business are extremely well informed on general politics—this is a peculiarity of ours: we do not say that a man who takes no interest in politics is a man who minds his own business; we say that he has no business here at all. We Athenians, in our own persons, take our decisions on policy or submit them to proper discussions: for we do not think that there is an incompatibility between words and deeds; the worst thing is to rush into action before the consequences have been properly debated...

I declare that our city is an education to Greece, and I declare that in my opinion each single on of our citizens, in all the manifold aspects of life, is able to show himself the rightful lord and owner of his own person, and do this, moreover, with exceptional grace and exceptional versatility."

Pre-Reading

Objective: Appreciating the moral and political views of ancient Greece.

Activity I

Read the excerpt and answer the questions that follow:

Pericles' funeral oration

As political and military leader of Athens, 460-429 B.C.E., Pericles delivered this eulogy at a mass funeral of troops who had died of plague in the early years of the Peloponnesian War. It is reported to be one of the great proclamations of the civic, aesthetic, moral, and personal virtues of the Athenian city-state.

"Our system of government does not copy the institutions of our neighbors. It is more the case of our being a model to others, than of our imitating anyone else. Our constitution is called a democracy because power is in the hands not of a minority but of the whole people. When it is a question of settling private disputes, everyone is equal before the law; when it is a question of putting one person before another in positions of public responsibility, what counts is not membership of a particular class, but the actual ability which the man possesses. No one, so long as he has it in him to be of service to the state, is kept in political obscurity because of poverty....

We [obey] those whom we put in positions of authority, and we obey the laws themselves, especially those which are for the protection of the oppressed, and those unwritten laws which it is an acknowledged shame to break....

When our work is over, we are in a position to enjoy all kinds of recreation for our spirits...all the good things from all over the world flow in to us, so that to us it seems just as natural to enjoy foreign goods as our own local products....

Our love of what is beautiful does not lead to extravagance; our love of the things of the mind does not make us soft. We regard wealth as something to be properly used, rather than as something to boast about. As for poverty, no one need be ashamed to admit it: the real shame is in not taking practical measures to escape from it. Here each individual is interested not only in his own affairs but in the affairs of the state as well: even those who are mostly occupied with their own business are extremely well informed on general politics—this is a peculiarity of ours: we do not say that a man who takes no interest in politics is a man who minds his own business; we say that he has no business here at all. We Athenians, in our own persons, take our decisions on policy or submit them to proper discussions: for we do not think that there is an incompatibility between words and deeds; the worst thing is to rush into action before the consequences have been properly debated...

I declare that our city is an education to Greece, and I declare that in my opinion each single on of our citizens, in all the manifold aspects of life, is able to show himself the rightful lord and owner of his own person, and do this, moreover, with exceptional grace and exceptional versatility."

Questions:

1.   Why is the Athenian government a democracy?

      All the people, not just a select group, hold power, and everyone is equal before the law.

2.   By what credentials is a person of public responsibility rated?

      A person is rated on ability and qualification, not on class.

3.   Does Athens practice trade with other city-states and nations?

      Yes, they trade all over the known world.

4.   How are wealth and poverty viewed?

      Wealth is used properly and not boasted about; poverty is nothing to be ashamed of as long as one strives to overcome it.

5.   How important is politics to the Athenians? Support your answer.

      Politics is very important. Everyone at least keeps up with current political events, and those who disregard politics are thought of as outsiders.

6.   Are the Athenians rash decision-makers? Why or why not?

      No. The Athenians ponder and discuss issues before a decision is made.

7.   How does Pericles view Athens and Athenians?

      He feels that Athens is a role model for Greece, and each citizen possesses a powerful sense of individualism, grace, and diverse knowledge.

Questions:

1. Why is the Athenian government a democracy?

2. By what credentials is a person of public responsibility rated?

3. Does Athens practice trade with other city-states and nations?

4. How are wealth and poverty viewed?

5. How important is politics to the Athenians? Support your answer.

6. Are the Athenians rash decision-makers? Why or why not?

7. How does Pericles view Athens and Athenians?

Activity II

Greek philosophers, such as Socrates and Plato, introduced questioning, methods of analysis and of teaching, and examinations of the purpose of life , which continue to command attention for their range and depth. Through incessant questions, they taught their students to be thoughtful but critical about the truths of others and about their own truths, and, after having reached their own conclusions, to live their own truths fully even if it meant death.

As a class, choose a difficult court case that has been in the newspapers lately, or create a situation with a difficult decision. Discuss what the ancient Greeks would do if found in a similar situation, and then discuss how they would reach their decision.

Answers will vary.
Examples of situations: if students were in a position to cheat on their boyfriends or girlfriends, or in a position to cheat on a test. The board game Scruples, with some of the adult cards perhaps removed, may help to generate discussion here. You should be prepared for committed religious beliefs to emerge, and have a strategy for defusing situations where some students may not respect each others' beliefs.

Activity II

Greek philosophers, such as Socrates and Plato, introduced questioning, methods of analysis and of teaching, and examinations of the purpose of life , which continue to command attention for their range and depth. Through incessant questions, they taught their students to be thoughtful but critical about the truths of others and about their own truths, and, after having reached their own conclusions, to live their own truths fully even if it meant death.

As a class, choose a difficult court case that has been in the newspapers lately, or create a situation with a difficult decision. Discuss what the ancient Greeks would do if found in a similar situation, and then discuss how they would reach their decision.

Pre-Reading

Objective: Exploring the fundamentals of ancient Greek and Roman culture.

Activity I

Greek and Roman art is found in sculpture, painting, pottery, and architecture. Sculptures include small figurines, life-size statues, and relief sculptures, located on the sides of buildings and tombstones. Paintings, such as murals or wallpaper, were used on walls as decoration for rooms. A good deal of pottery survived through the ages, much of it painted, which offers clues to the culture of that time. Architecture includes houses, religious buildings, theaters, and stadiums.

Research the art and architecture of the Greek and Roman civilizations. The Internet is an excellent tool for locating pictures and facts about the styles. Begin a hunt to collect elements of Greek and Roman art and architecture. Go through newspapers and magazines for pictures, and cut them out. Go on a walk and take pictures of building architecture. Some suggestions of architectural items to look for are the columns found in front of schools, post offices, and houses. Many churches are built in a Romanesque style, and sometimes park or neighborhood entrances will have triumphal arches. Look for cobblestone streets in historic areas. Gather your pictures and create a collage.

Pre-Reading

Objective: Exploring the fundamentals of ancient Greek and Roman culture.

Activity I

Greek and Roman art is found in sculpture, painting, pottery, and architecture. Sculptures include small figurines, life-size statues, and relief sculptures, located on the sides of buildings and tombstones. Paintings, such as murals or wallpaper, were used on walls as decoration for rooms. A good deal of pottery survived through the ages, much of it painted, which offers clues to the culture of that time. Architecture includes houses, religious buildings, theaters, and stadiums.

Research the art and architecture of the Greek and Roman civilizations. The Internet is an excellent tool for locating pictures and facts about the styles. Begin a hunt to collect elements of Greek and Roman art and architecture. Go through newspapers and magazines for pictures, and cut them out. Go on a walk and take pictures of building architecture. Some suggestions of architectural items to look for are the columns found in front of schools, post offices, and houses. Many churches are built in a Romanesque style, and sometimes park or neighborhood entrances will have triumphal arches. Look for cobblestone streets in historic areas. Gather your pictures and create a collage.

Pre-Reading

Objective: Logging historical events on a timeline.

Activity I

1.   Read the following summary on the life of Alexander the Great. Use the information to fill in the appropriate dates and events on the timeline.

          Alexander the Great was born in Macedonia, northern Greece, in 356 B.C.E. By the time Alexander was a teenager, his father, King Philip, had begun a systematic policy of expanding his kingdom. While still in his teens, Alexander commanded a Macedonian legion at the battle of Chaeronea in 338. King Philip was killed in 336, and Alexander ascended to the Macedonian throne.

          In 334, Alexander was ready to cross into Asia, where his first major victory came at Granicus. Alexander's main opponent was the Persian King Darius III, whose kingdom stretched from Egypt and the Mediterranean into India and central Asia. Alexander defeated Darius during three major engagements. He conquered Persian forces at Turkey in 334. Alexander marched eastward with 35,000 Greek troops, routing the 300,000-man Persian army at Issus in 333, and forced Darius into flight. Alexander's final victory over the Persians was at Gaugamela (Iraq) in 331. Having captured the heartland of the Persian Empire, Alexander set off to conquer the eastern half as well. He proceeded to capture the Indus River valley in the east and Sogdiana, across the Oxus River, in the northeast. He defeated King Porus at the river Hydaspes (India) in 326. After this battle, under the persuasion of his troops, Alexander returned to his new capital in Babylon. Those who returned with Alexander covered over 20,000 miles within a period of roughly ten years. In 323, Alexander contracted a fever and died at the age of thirty-three.

Timeline: Alexander the Great

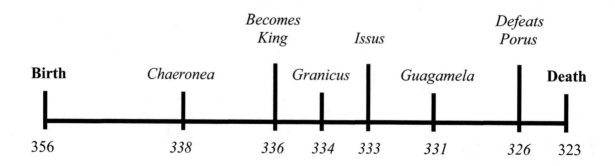

Pre-Reading

Objective: Logging historical events on a timeline.

Activity I

1. Read the following summary on the life of Alexander the Great. Use the information to fill in the appropriate dates and events on the timeline.

> Alexander the Great was born in Macedonia, northern Greece, in 356 B.C.E. By the time Alexander was a teenager, his father, King Philip, had begun a systematic policy of expanding his kingdom. While still in his teens, Alexander commanded a Macedonian legion at the battle of Chaeronea in 338. King Philip was killed in 336, and Alexander ascended to the Macedonian throne.
>
> In 334, Alexander was ready to cross into Asia, where his first major victory came at Granicus. Alexander's main opponent was the Persian King Darius III, whose kingdom stretched from Egypt and the Mediterranean into India and central Asia. Alexander defeated Darius during three major engagements. He conquered Persian forces at Turkey in 334. Alexander marched eastward with 35,000 Greek troops, routing the 300,000-man Persian army at Issus in 333, and forced Darius into flight. Alexander's final victory over the Persians was at Gaugamela (Iraq) in 331. Having captured the heartland of the Persian Empire, Alexander set off to conquer the eastern half as well. He proceeded to capture the Indus River valley in the east and Sogdiana, across the Oxus River, in the northeast. He defeated King Porus at the river Hydaspes (India) in 326. After this battle, under the persuasion of his troops, Alexander returned to his new capital in Babylon. Those who returned with Alexander covered over 20,000 miles within a period of roughly ten years. In 323, Alexander contracted a fever and died at the age of thirty-three.

Timeline: Alexander the Great

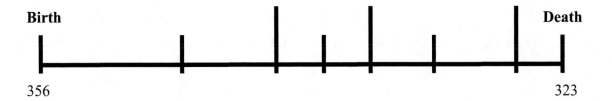

Birth   **Death**

356   323

2.   Use the Internet to locate an ancient map of the regions Alexander the Great conquered. The map needs to include the areas of Greece, the land around the Mediterranean Sea, and eastward to Western India. An excellent site to find a map is http://killeenroos.com/link/maps.html . Print a copy of the map, and trace the route Alexander's army took from Chaeronea to Hydaspes, and back to Babylon. Mark the sites of his battles along the route.

2.   Use the Internet to locate an ancient map of the regions Alexander the Great conquered. The map needs to include the areas of Greece, the land around the Mediterranean Sea, and eastward to Western India. An excellent site to find a map is http://killeenroos.com/link/maps.html . Print a copy of the map, and trace the route Alexander's army took from Chaeronea to Hydaspes, and back to Babylon. Mark the sites of his battles along the route.

Chapter 1
Reading for Details
Character Comprehension

Objective: Identifying characters through their distinguishing traits.

Activity I

Greek culture began as early as the eighth century B.C.E., and it continued to flourish in art, architecture, and literature until the "Golden Age" of the fifth century B.C.E. Man lived in close affiliation with nature, and this relationship, in conjunction with curiosity about the cosmos, the creation of man, and life after death, led to the birth of mythology. The Greek gods of Olympus are painted with human characteristics and emotions, while at the same time possessing immortality and divine powers.

Hamilton gives detailed accounts of the Olympian gods, including gods of the water, earth, and underworld. Use the clues provided to complete the crossword puzzle on the following page.

Activity II

Greek art and literature greatly influenced Roman culture and, as a result, the Olympian gods merged with the Roman deities. With the exception of Apollo and Pluto, the Greek gods were given Roman names. The Roman deities embraced distinct and vivid personalities. Match the following Greek gods with their corresponding Roman counterparts.

Greek gods   **Roman gods**

1.   Artemis   _____   A. Pluto
2.   Hera   _____   B. Jupiter
3.   Ares   _____   C. Bacchus
4.   Zeus   _____   D. Juno
5.   Hades   _____   E. Mercury
6.   Athena   _____   F. Neptune
7.   Aphrodite _____   G. Mars
8.   Demeter   _____   H. Diana
9.   Poseidon   _____   I. Minerva
10. Hermes   _____   J. Venus
11. Dionysus   _____   K. Ceres

Answer Key
1.	*H*	*5.*	*A*	*9.*	*F*
2.	*D*	*6.*	*I*	*10.*	*E*
3.	*G*	*7.*	*J*	*11.*	*C*
4.	*B*	*8.*	*K*		

Chapter 1
Reading for Details
Character Comprehension

Objective: Identifying characters through their distinguishing traits.

Activity I

Greek culture began as early as the eighth century B.C.E., and it continued to flourish in art, architecture, and literature until the "Golden Age" of the fifth century B.C.E. Man lived in close affiliation with nature, and this relationship, in conjunction with curiosity about the cosmos, the creation of man, and life after death, led to the birth of mythology. The Greek gods of Olympus are painted with human characteristics and emotions, while at the same time possessing immortality and divine powers.

Hamilton gives detailed accounts of the Olympian gods, including gods of the water, earth, and underworld. Use the clues provided to complete the crossword puzzle on the following page.

Activity II

Greek art and literature greatly influenced Roman culture and, as a result, the Olympian gods merged with the Roman deities. With the exception of Apollo and Pluto, the Greek gods were given Roman names. The Roman deities embraced distinct and vivid personalities. Match the following Greek gods with their corresponding Roman counterparts.

Greek gods		**Roman gods**
1. Artemis	_____	A. Pluto
2. Hera	_____	B. Jupiter
3. Ares	_____	C. Bacchus
4. Zeus	_____	D. Juno
5. Hades	_____	E. Mercury
6. Athena	_____	F. Neptune
7. Aphrodite	_____	G. Mars
8. Demeter	_____	H. Diana
9. Poseidon	_____	I. Minerva
10. Hermes	_____	J. Venus
11. Dionysus	_____	K. Ceres

Across

2   Goddess of the rainbow
3   Goddess of marriage
5   God of love
7   The elder gods
11   Goddess of battle and wisdom
12   Goddess of love and beauty
15   Goddess of youth
16   God of the shepherds
17   Father of Zeus
18   Goddess of the hearth
19   God of the sea

Down

1   Three sisters; Incarnation of
       grace and beauty
4   Goddess of hunting
6   Queen of the underworld
8   God of the vine
9   God of the underworld
10   The mightiest god
11   God of war
13   God of fire
14   God of art and truth
15   Messenger of the gods

Across

2	Goddess of the rainbow
3	Goddess of marriage
5	God of love
7	The elder gods
11	Goddess of battle and wisdom
12	Goddess of love and beauty
15	Goddess of youth
16	God of the shepherds
17	Father of Zeus
18	Goddess of the hearth
19	God of the sea

8	God of the vine
9	God of the underworld
10	The mightiest god
11	God of war
13	God of fire
14	God of art and truth
15	Messenger of the gods

Down

1	Three sisters; Incarnation of grace and beauty
4	Goddess of hunting
6	Queen of the underworld

Answer key

Across

2. *Iris*
3. *Hera*
5. *Cupid*
7. *Titans*
11. *Athena*
12. *Aphrodite*
15. *Hebe*
16. *Pan*
17. *Cronus*
18. *Hestia*
19. *Poseidon*

Down

1. *Graces*
4. *Artemis*
6. *Persephone*
8. *Dionysus*
9. *Hades*
10. *Zeus*
11. *Ares*
13. *Hephaestus*
14. *Apollo*
15. *Hermes*

Chapter 2
Visualization
Characterization

Objective: Interpreting and visualizing the thoughts and actions of a character.

Activity I

A festival is held every year to revere Demeter, the goddess of corn, to give thanks for a fruitful harvest. Demeter is not always a happy goddess of summertime because her tale also contains pain and sorrow. The myth of the kidnapping of Persephone, Demeter's daughter, is used to explain the winter months, when all the growth of earth must end with the coming of cold.

Read Demeter's tale, taken from one of the earliest Homeric Hymns. Based on the text, choose at least five traits you believe Demeter possesses.

1.____	Wisdom	11.____	Greediness
2.____	Stubbornness	12.____	Shrewdness
3.____	Bravery	13.____	Sorrow
4.____	Callousness	14.____	Vengefulness
5.____	Understanding	15.____	Luck
6.____	Reliability	16.____	Persistence
7.____	Loyalty	17.____	Love
8.____	Kindness	18.____	Reason
9.____	Thoughtfulness	19.____	Diplomacy
10.____	Honesty	20.____	Intelligence

More than five responses are correct, so answers will vary.
stubbornness, kindness, sorrow, vengefulness, persistence

Select any two of the characteristics you chose and give supporting quotations from the text. For example, a passage to support the selection "stubbornness" might be:

> "He [Zeus] sent the gods to Demeter, one after another, to try to turn her from her anger, but she listened to none of them." (Pg.53)

Chapter 2
Visualization
Characterization

Objective: Interpreting and visualizing the thoughts and actions of a character.

Activity I

A festival is held every year to revere Demeter, the goddess of corn, to give thanks for a fruitful harvest. Demeter is not always a happy goddess of summertime because her tale also contains pain and sorrow. The myth of the kidnapping of Persephone, Demeter's daughter, is used to explain the winter months, when all the growth of earth must end with the coming of cold.

Read Demeter's tale, taken from one of the earliest Homeric Hymns. Based on the text, choose at least five traits you believe Demeter possesses.

1.____	Wisdom	11.____	Greediness
2.____	Stubbornness	12.____	Shrewdness
3.____	Bravery	13.____	Sorrow
4.____	Callousness	14.____	Vengefulness
5.____	Understanding	15.____	Luck
6.____	Reliability	16.____	Persistence
7.____	Loyalty	17.____	Love
8.____	Kindness	18.____	Reason
9.____	Thoughtfulness	19.____	Diplomacy
10.____	Honesty	20.____	Intelligence

Select any two of the characteristics you chose and give supporting quotations from the text. For example, a passage to support the selection "stubbornness" might be:

> "He [Zeus] sent the gods to Demeter, one after another, to try to turn her
> from her anger, but she listened to none of them." (Pg.53)

Activity II

Myths surrounding Dionysus, the god of the vine, portray merriment and tragedy. Celebration ensues with the harvest of grapes, but winter brings the grief of bare vines. Drinking wine can enhance confidence and happiness, but it can also bring anger and degradation.

Dionysus performs acts of kindness and cruelty upon the humans he encounters. The following excerpt, though, is an example of the darker side of Dionysus. Visualize the events that take place in this passage, and draw a picture illustrating the scene. Create a caption that you believe depicts your artwork accurately.

> "Fragrant wine ran in streams down the deck; a vine with many clusters spread out over the sail; a dark green ivy-plant twined around the mast like a garland, with flowers in it and lovely fruits. Terror-stricken, the pirates ordered the helmsman to put in to land. Too late, for as they spoke their captive [Dionysus] became a lion, roaring and glaring terribly. At that, they leaped overboard and instantly were changed into dolphins, all except the good helmsman." (Pg.57)

An example of a caption: "The Wrath of Dionysus."

Activity II

Myths surrounding Dionysus, the god of the vine, portray merriment and tragedy. Celebration ensues with the harvest of grapes, but winter brings the grief of bare vines. Drinking wine can enhance confidence and happiness, but it can also bring anger and degradation.

Dionysus performs acts of kindness and cruelty upon the humans he encounters. The following excerpt, though, is an example of the darker side of Dionysus. Visualize the events that take place in this passage, and draw a picture illustrating the scene. Create a caption that you believe depicts your artwork accurately.

"Fragrant wine ran in streams down the deck; a vine with many clusters spread out over the sail; a dark green ivy-plant twined around the mast like a garland, with flowers in it and lovely fruits. Terror-stricken, the pirates ordered the helmsman to put in to land. Too late, for as they spoke their captive [Dionysus] became a lion, roaring and glaring terribly. At that, they leaped overboard and instantly were changed into dolphins, all except the good helmsman." (Pg.57)

Chapter 3
Comparison
Tragic Flaw
Theme

Objective: Recognizing the common tragic flaw and theme in similar stories.

Activity I

Read the following excerpts from *Mythology* and the *Holy Bible*, both about the first woman created. Based on these excerpts, complete the following comparison chart.

Excerpt One: *Mythology* by Edith Hamilton

> "Another story about Pandora is that the source of all misfortune was not her wicked nature, but only her curiosity. The gods presented her with a box into which each had put something harmful, and forbade her ever to open it. Then they sent her to Epimetheus, who took her gladly although Prometheus had warned him never to accept anything from Zeus. He took her, and afterward when that dangerous thing, a woman, was his, he understood how good his brother's advice had been. For Pandora, like all women, was possessed of a lively curiosity. She *had* to know what was in the box. One day she lifted the lid—and out flew plagues innumerable, sorrow and mischief for mankind. In terror Pandora clapped the lid down, but too late." (Pg. 74)

Chapter 3
Comparison
Tragic Flaw
Theme

Objective: Recognizing the common tragic flaw and theme in similar stories.

Activity I

Read the following excerpts from *Mythology* and the *Holy Bible*, both about the first woman created. Based on these excerpts, complete the following comparison chart.

Excerpt One: *Mythology* by Edith Hamilton

"Another story about Pandora is that the source of all misfortune was not her wicked nature, but only her curiosity. The gods presented her with a box into which each had put something harmful, and forbade her ever to open it. Then they sent her to Epimetheus, who took her gladly although Prometheus had warned him never to accept anything from Zeus. He took her, and afterward when that dangerous thing, a woman, was his, he understood how good his brother's advice had been. For Pandora, like all women, was possessed of a lively curiosity. She *had* to know what was in the box. One day she lifted the lid—and out flew plagues innumerable, sorrow and mischief for mankind. In terror Pandora clapped the lid down, but too late." (Pg. 74)

Excerpt Two: *Holy Bible*, King James Version, Book of Genesis

"And the woman [Eve] said unto the serpent, We may eat of the fruit of the trees of the garden: But of the fruit of the tree which *is* in the midst of the garden, God hath said, Ye shall not eat of it, neither shall ye touch it lest ye die. And the serpent said unto the woman, Ye shall not surely die: For God doth know that in the day ye eat thereof, then your eyes shall be opened, and ye shall be as gods, knowing good and evil. And when the woman saw that the tree *was* good for food, and that it *was* pleasant to the eyes, and a tree to be desired to make *one* wise, she took of the fruit thereof, and did eat, and gave also unto her husband with her; and he did eat." (Genesis 3:2-6)

Comparison Chart

Question	Excerpt One	Excerpt Two
What tragic flaw does the woman possess?	*curiosity*	*curiosity, thirst for knowledge*
Is the story religious?	*yes*	*yes*
Why was this story written?	*explanation of the plagues of earth*	*explanation of mankind's knowledge of good and evil*
How is the woman viewed?	*dangerous, deceitful, mischievous*	*disobedient, easily persuaded*
What is the theme of the story?	*women are evil and cannot be trusted ; mankind is not perfect*	*women are emotional and unreliable; mankind is not perfect*
Why is a woman blamed for the great hardships released?	*ancient civilization did not hold women in high esteem*	*ancient civilization did not hold women in high esteem*

Activity II

The story of the flood is also found in several ancient narratives of world literature. Tablets containing portions of *The Epic of Gilgamesh*, a poem of antiquity, was discovered at sites throughout the Middle East in 1872. *Gilgamesh* developed over a period of nearly a thousand years, and vanished when the civilizations of the Greeks, Hebrews, and Romans had only just developed beyond their infancy. Until the story was rediscovered and published, everyone believed that the Biblical story of Noah and the great flood was original and unique.

Read the next three excerpts, all relating to the story of the great flood, and answer the following questions.

Excerpt Two: *Holy Bible*, **King James Version, Book of Genesis**

"And the woman [Eve] said unto the serpent, We may eat of the fruit of the trees of the garden: But of the fruit of the tree which *is* in the midst of the garden, God hath said, Ye shall not eat of it, neither shall ye touch it lest ye die. And the serpent said unto the woman, Ye shall not surely die: For God doth know that in the day ye eat thereof, then your eyes shall be opened, and ye shall be as gods, knowing good and evil. And when the woman saw that the tree *was* good for food, and that it *was* pleasant to the eyes, and a tree to be desired to make *one* wise, she took of the fruit thereof, and did eat, and gave also unto her husband with her; and he did eat." (Genesis 3:2-6)

Comparison Chart

Question	Excerpt One	Excerpt Two
What tragic flaw does the woman possess?		
Is the story religious?		
Why was this story written?		
How is the woman viewed?		
What is the theme of the story?		
Why is a woman blamed for the great hardships released?		

Activity II

The story of the flood is also found in several ancient narratives of world literature. Tablets containing portions of *The Epic of Gilgamesh*, a poem of antiquity, was discovered at sites throughout the Middle East in 1872. *Gilgamesh* developed over a period of nearly a thousand years, and vanished when the civilizations of the Greeks, Hebrews, and Romans had only just developed beyond their infancy. Until the story was rediscovered and published, everyone believed that the Biblical story of Noah and the great flood was original and unique.

Excerpt One: *Mythology* by Edith Hamilton

"All over the earth men grew so wicked that finally Zeus determined to destroy them. He decided
To mingle storm and tempest over boundless earth
And make an utter end of mortal man.
He sent the flood. He called upon his brother, the God of the Sea, to help him, and together, with torrents of rain from heaven and rivers loosed upon the earth, the two drowned the land... After it had rained through, nine days and nine nights, there came drifting to that spot what looked to be a great wooden chest... The wisest person in all the universe, Prometheus had well been able to protect his own family. He knew the flood would come, and he had bidden his son to build the chest, store it with provisions, and embark in it with his wife." (Pgs. 76-77)

Excerpt Two: *Holy Bible*, King James Version, Book of Genesis

"And God saw that the wickedness of man was great in the earth, and that every imagination of the thoughts of his heart was only evil continually. And it repented the Lord that he had made man on the earth, and it grieved him at his heart. And the Lord said, I will destroy man whom I have created from the face of the earth; both man, and beast, and the creeping thing, and the fowls of the air; for it repenteth me that I have made them. But Noah found grace in the eyes of the Lord. . .And God said unto Noah, The end of all flesh is come before me, for the earth is filled with violence through them,; and, behold, I will destroy them with the earth. Make thee an ark of gopher wood. . . And, behold, I, even I, do bring a flood of waters upon the earth, to destroy all flesh, wherein is the breath of life, from under heaven; and every thing that is in the earth shall die. But with thee will I establish my covenant; and thou shalt come into the ark, thou, and thy sons, and thy wife, and thy sons wives with thee." (Genesis 3:5-18)

Excerpt Three: *The Epic of Gilgamesh*, 2500-1500 B.C.E.

"In those days the world teemed, the people multiplied, the world bellowed like a wild bull, and the great god was aroused by the clamour. Enlil heard the clamour and he said to the gods in council, 'The uproar of mankind is intolerable and sleep is no longer possible by reason of the babble.' So the gods agreed to exterminate mankind. Enlil did this, but Ea because of his oath warned me [Utnapishtim] in a dream. He whispered their words, '...tear down your house and build a boat, abandon possessions and look for life, despite worldly goods and save your soul alive. Tear down your house, I say, and build a boat.'...For six days and six nights the winds blew, torrent and tempest and flood overwhelmed the world, tempest and flood raged together like warring hosts. When the seventh day dawned the storm from the south subsided, the sea grew calm, the flood was stilled; I looked at the face of the word and there was silence, all mankind was turned to clay." (Part 5)

Answers may vary.

1.   What parallels can you find in these excerpts?
        angry god, cataclysmic flood, one family survives in an ark

2.   What is the reason for the creation of these stories?
        religious explanation for historical event, oral tradition, fear or curiosity of unknown

Read the next three excerpts, all relating to the story of the great flood, and answer the following questions.

Excerpt One: *Mythology* by Edith Hamilton

"All over the earth men grew so wicked that finally Zeus determined to destroy them. He decided
To mingle storm and tempest over boundless earth
And make an utter end of mortal man.
He sent the flood. He called upon his brother, the God of the Sea, to help him, and together, with torrents of rain from heaven and rivers loosed upon the earth, the two drowned the land… After it had rained through, nine days and nine nights, there came drifting to that spot what looked to be a great wooden chest… The wisest person in all the universe, Prometheus had well been able to protect his own family. He knew the flood would come, and he had bidden his son to build the chest, store it with provisions, and embark in it with his wife." (Pgs. 76-77)

Excerpt Two: *Holy Bible*, King James Version, Book of Genesis

"And God saw that the wickedness of man was great in the earth, and that every imagination of the thoughts of his heart was only evil continually. And it repented the Lord that he had made man on the earth, and it grieved him at his heart. And the Lord said, I will destroy man whom I have created from the face of the earth; both man, and beast, and the creeping thing, and the fowls of the air; for it repenteth me that I have made them. But Noah found grace in the eyes of the Lord. . .And God said unto Noah, The end of all flesh is come before me, for the earth is filled with violence through them,; and, behold, I will destroy them with the earth. Make thee an ark of gopher wood. . . And, behold, I, even I, do bring a flood of waters upon the earth, to destroy all flesh, wherein is the breath of life, from under heaven; and every thing that is in the earth shall die. But with thee will I establish my covenant; and thou shalt come into the ark, thou, and thy sons, and thy wife, and thy sons wives with thee." (Genesis 3:5-18)

Excerpt Three: *The Epic of Gilgamesh*, 2500-1500 B.C.E.

"In those days the world teemed, the people multiplied, the world bellowed like a wild bull, and the great god was aroused by the clamour. Enlil heard the clamour and he said to the gods in council, 'The uproar of mankind is intolerable and sleep is no longer possible by reason of the babble.' So the gods agreed to exterminate mankind. Enlil did this, but Ea because of his oath warned me [Utnapishtim] in a dream. He whispered their words, '…tear down your house and build a boat, abandon possessions and look for life, despite worldly goods and save your soul alive. Tear down your house, I say, and build a boat.'…For six days and six nights the winds blew, torrent and tempest and flood overwhelmed the world, tempest and flood raged together like warring hosts. When the seventh day dawned the storm from the south subsided, the sea grew calm, the flood was stilled; I looked at the face of the word and there was silence, all mankind was turned to clay." (Part 5)

3. Why do you suppose a natural disaster is used to punish mankind for wickedness?

catastrophic event can only be an act of god, nature controlled by god

4. What kind of people created these stories?

imaginative, religious, story-tellers, observers of nature

5. What is the common theme found in these stories?

evil will be punished, god is always watching, goodness will endure

1.   What parallels can you find in these excerpts?

2.   What is the reason for the creation of these stories?

3.   Why do you suppose a natural disaster is used to punish mankind for wickedness?

4.   What kind of people created these stories?

5.   What is the common theme found in these stories?

Chapter 4
Group Work
Dramatization
Inference
Dialogue

Objective: Inferring the thoughts and feelings of a character.

Activity I

Ovid, an ancient Roman writer, gives a detailed account of Zeus' approach to Io in *The Metamorphoses*.

> "Now it was Jove [Zeus] who caught sight of Io; she was returning from her father's stream, and Jove had said: 'O virgin, you indeed would merit Jove and will make any man you wed—whoever he may be—most glad. But now it's time for you to seek the shade of those deep woods' (and here he pointed toward a nearby forest); 'for the sun is high—at its midcourse; such heat can't be defied. And do not be afraid to find yourself alone among the haunts of savage beasts: within the forest depths you can be sure of safety, for your guardian is a god—and I am not a common deity: for I am he who holds within his hand the heavens' scepter: I am he who hurls the roaming thunderbolts. So do not flee!' But even as he spoke, she'd left behind the pasturelands of Lerna, and the plains around Lyrceus' peak, fields thick with trees. Then with a veil of heavy fog, the god concealed a vast expanse of land; Jove stopped her flight; he raped chaste Io." (verses 202-223)

Zeus's attack upon Io ruins her life. Transformed into a heifer, Io suffers humiliation, is estranged from her family, and becomes imprisoned by Hera. Suppose, after being rescued and restored to her human form, Io decides to seek retribution for the injustices she endured.

The class will perform a mock trial in which Io is suing Zeus. As a class, decide what the accusation(s) against Zeus will be. Then, divide into four groups: prosecution, defense, witnesses, and jury. Each group must prepare its role.

Prosecution: The characters to be represented are Io and her lawyers. Determine the retribution sought, collect supporting evidence from the text and the paragraph above, form questions to ask the witnesses, including cross-examination, and compose a closing argument for the court.

Defense: The characters to be represented are Zeus and his lawyers. Build a defense against possible accusations, gather evidence, form questions to ask the witnesses including, cross-examination, and compose a closing argument for the court.

Witnesses: The characters to be represented are Hera, Prometheus, Hermes, and Argus. The witnesses must be knowledgeable of the parts their characters play in the story.

Chapter 4
Group Work
Dramatization
Inference
Dialogue

Objective: Inferring the thoughts and feelings of a character.

Activity I

Ovid, an ancient Roman writer, gives a detailed account of Zeus' approach to Io in *The Metamorphoses*.

> "Now it was Jove [Zeus] who caught sight of Io; she was returning from her father's stream, and Jove had said: 'O virgin, you indeed would merit Jove and will make any man you wed—whoever he may be—most glad. But now it's time for you to seek the shade of those deep woods' (and here he pointed toward a nearby forest); 'for the sun is high—at its midcourse; such heat can't be defied. And do not be afraid to find yourself alone among the haunts of savage beasts: within the forest depths you can be sure of safety, for your guardian is a god—and I am not a common deity: for I am he who holds within his hand the heavens' scepter: I am he who hurls the roaming thunderbolts. So do not flee!' But even as he spoke, she'd left behind the pasturelands of Lerna, and the plains around Lyrceus' peak, fields thick with trees. Then with a veil of heavy fog, the god concealed a vast expanse of land; Jove stopped her flight; he raped chaste Io." (verses 202-223)

Zeus's attack upon Io ruins her life. Transformed into a heifer, Io suffers humiliation, is estranged from her family, and becomes imprisoned by Hera. Suppose, after being rescued and restored to her human form, Io decides to seek retribution for the injustices she endured.

The class will perform a mock trial in which Io is suing Zeus. As a class, decide what the accusation(s) against Zeus will be. Then, divide into four groups: prosecution, defense, witnesses, and jury. Each group must prepare its role.

Prosecution: The characters to be represented are Io and her lawyers. Determine the retribution sought, collect supporting evidence from the text and the paragraph above, form questions to ask the witnesses, including cross-examination, and compose a closing argument for the court.

Defense: The characters to be represented are Zeus and his lawyers. Build a defense against possible accusations, gather evidence, form questions to ask the witnesses including, cross-examination, and compose a closing argument for the court.

Witnesses: The characters to be represented are Hera, Prometheus, Hermes, and Argus. The witnesses must be knowledgeable of the parts their characters play in the story.

Jury: The number of students left over after the other roles have been filled determines the jury size. Each jury member will listen closely to both sides and draw a two-column chart: one side for guilt and one side for innocence. Log the evidence and any observations accordingly.

The trial will follow modern laws and proceed like that of a normal court hearing. At the end, the jury decides if Zeus was justified in his actions.

Examples of lawsuit accusations are stalking, rape, and assault.
Questions may deal with the cause of Zeus's actions, individual rights, or the extent of influence or power religion has in life.

Activity II

Hera unjustifiably punishes Echo so that the nymph can only repeat what is said to her. As a result of this punishment, Echo is unable to converse freely with Narcissus, and she is shunned. Echo's unrequited love for Narcissus causes her to pine away until only her voice remains.

Imagine that Narcissus, regardless of his vanity and Echo's handicap, does not turn her away. As a result, the two characters fall in love. With this ending in mind, complete the following dialogue. Be sure to follow Echo's speaking style.

Narcissus:	Is anyone here?
Echo:	Here - here.
Narcissus:	Why don't you come out?
Echo:	Come out!
Narcissus:	You're lovely to look at.
Echo:	You're lovely to look at.

Answers will vary.
Example of a continuing conversation:

Narcissus:	*Is anything more beautiful than you?*
Echo:	*You—you.*
Narcissus:	*Your name is Echo, right?*
Echo:	*Right.*
Narcissus:	*Please don't go. Stay with me.*
Echo:	*Stay with me.*
Narcissus:	*How long can we last? A day, a week, or forever?*
Echo:	*Forever—forever.*
Narcissus:	*So be it. You will always have my love.*
Echo:	*My love.*

Jury: The number of students left over after the other roles have been filled determines the jury size. Each jury member will listen closely to both sides and draw a two-column chart: one side for guilt and one side for innocence. Log the evidence and any observations accordingly.

The trial will follow modern laws and proceed like that of a normal court hearing. At the end, the jury decides if Zeus was justified in his actions.

Activity II

Hera unjustifiably punishes Echo so that the nymph can only repeat what is said to her. As a result of this punishment, Echo is unable to converse freely with Narcissus, and she is shunned. Echo's unrequited love for Narcissus causes her to pine away until only her voice remains.

Imagine that Narcissus, regardless of his vanity and Echo's handicap, does not turn her away. As a result, the two characters fall in love. With this ending in mind, complete the following dialogue. Be sure to follow Echo's speaking style.

Narcissus:	Is anyone here?
Echo:	Here - here.
Narcissus:	Why don't you come out?
Echo:	Come out!
Narcissus:	You're lovely to look at.
Echo:	You're lovely to look at.

Chapter 5
Theme

Objective: Extracting an intended theme or lesson from a story.

Activity I

1. The classical story of Cupid and Psyche deals with the hardships true love must sometimes endure. Cupid's mother, Venus, is extremely jealous of Psyche, and she orders the mortal princess to complete a series of tasks. Successfully accomplishing the difficult chores, Psyche is once again united with her husband, only now as a goddess.

    Every test Psyche undertakes has an ethical theme. Complete the following chart by supplying the virtue or characteristic pertaining to the task. The first one has been done as an example.

Virtue Chart

Task	Required Virtue
Diligently separate and sort a great number of tiny seeds.	patience
Collect gold fleece from the fierce sheep.	*wit, ingenuity*
Fill a flask with black water from the river Styx.	*bravery, perseverance*
Travel to Hades and have a box filled by Proserpine.	*courage, integrity*

Answers will vary.
Acceptable answers are traits that display a strong, determined, and virtuous character.

2. Psyche and Venus compete in a battle of wills over Cupid. Write a brief paragraph comparing traits of the two women.

    Answers will vary.
    Some similar traits: beauty, vanity, perseverance, intelligence, and strong love for Cupid.
    Some different traits:, Psyche displays patience, regret, and kindness, while Venus appears impatient, jealous, and cruel.

3. Cupid represents love and Psyche means spirit or soul. Based on these points, what do you believe is the theme of the story? Support your answer.

    Answers will vary.
    Love and the soul have sought each other out and, through trials and tribulations, created an eternal union.

Chapter 5
Theme

Objective: Extracting an intended theme or lesson from a story.

Activity I

1.   The classical story of Cupid and Psyche deals with the hardships true love must sometimes endure. Cupid's mother, Venus, is extremely jealous of Psyche, and she orders the mortal princess to complete a series of tasks. Successfully accomplishing the difficult chores, Psyche is once again united with her husband, only now as a goddess.

   Every test Psyche undertakes has an ethical theme. Complete the following chart by supplying the virtue or characteristic pertaining to the task. The first one has been done as an example.

Virtue Chart

Task	Required Virtue
Diligently separate and sort a great number of tiny seeds.	patience
Collect gold fleece from the fierce sheep.	
Fill a flask with black water from the river Styx.	
Travel to Hades and have a box filled by Proserpine.	

2.   Psyche and Venus compete in a battle of wills over Cupid. Write a brief paragraph comparing traits of the two women.

3.   Cupid represents love and Psyche means spirit or soul. Based on these points, what do you believe is the theme of the story? Support your answer.

Activity II

Write a letter of apology from Psyche to Cupid explaining the reason for spying on him while he slept and why it was a mistake. Persuade Cupid to forgive and forget the dreadful event. Make sure you reference what has happened between them, as explained in the text.

Answers will vary.
Psyche spies on Cupid because her sisters heighten her fear and curiosity about Cupid's true identity and appearance. As a result, Psyche destroys all faith and trust with her husband. Sample letter:

My Dearest Husband,

Words cannot express the regret I feel for the wrong I have committed. In faith, I meant no malice or harm towards you. I hope, upon hearing my case, you can find it in your heart to forgive me.

Our marriage has been pure bliss since the day it began, and the care you bestowed upon me exceeded my every expectation. For this reason, I could not understand your insistence in hiding your identity. Indeed, your advice was sound when you warned me not to heed my sisters' words. No matter how hard I tried to ignore their arguments, my sisters eventually destroyed my resolve and cast doubt into my heart. In yielding to this flaw—curiosity—I have destroyed the euphoric union we shared.

Should it take a thousand years, I will persevere to regain your love and trust. Give me a task, any task, and it shall be done. From the depths of my soul, I beseech you to free me from this self-inflicted agony. My love, please forgive me.

Yours ever,
Psyche

Activity II

Write a letter of apology from Psyche to Cupid explaining the reason for spying on him while he slept and why it was a mistake. Persuade Cupid to forgive and forget the dreadful event. Make sure you reference what has happened between them, as explained in the text.

Chapter 6
Group Work
Setting
Narrator

Objective: Rewriting and critiquing the setting, narration, and conclusion of a story.

Activity I

Pyramus and Thisbe, the young Babylonian lovers, share a forbidden love that is separated by a wall. While attempting to elope, Pyramus mistakenly thinks Thisbe has been killed and rashly commits suicide, whereupon Thisbe in despair stabs herself. The climax in Shakespeare's *Romeo and Juliet* closely resembles Pyramus and Thisbe: Romeo believes Juliet to be dead and kills himself; Juliet discovers him and similarly takes her life. Each story consists of the same material, depicting romantic love and tragic destiny.

The theme of star-crossed lovers is universal because the story can be told in any time and place. The story of ill-fated lovers from feuding families has been retold countless times, and now it is your turn to tell the tale. Using third-person narration, rewrite the love story of Pyramus and Thisbe. Choose a setting by deciding when (past, present, or future) and where the story takes place. Be as creative as you wish.

Answers will vary.

Chapter 6
Group Work
Setting
Narrator

Objective: Rewriting and critiquing the setting, narration, and conclusion of a story.

Activity I

Pyramus and Thisbe, the young Babylonian lovers, share a forbidden love that is separated by a wall. While attempting to elope, Pyramus mistakenly thinks Thisbe has been killed and rashly commits suicide, whereupon Thisbe in despair stabs herself. The climax in Shakespeare's *Romeo and Juliet* closely resembles Pyramus and Thisbe: Romeo believes Juliet to be dead and kills himself; Juliet discovers him and similarly takes her life. Each story consists of the same material, depicting romantic love and tragic destiny.

The theme of star-crossed lovers is universal because the story can be told in any time and place. The story of ill-fated lovers from feuding families has been retold countless times, and now it is your turn to tell the tale. Using third-person narration, rewrite the love story of Pyramus and Thisbe. Choose a setting by deciding when (past, present, or future) and where the story takes place. Be as creative as you wish.

Activity II

Orpheus possesses a musical gift that is rivaled only by the gods, and his power has no limits when he plays and sings. The premature death of his wife, Eurydice, prompts Orpheus to travel to the underworld in an attempt to recover her. With imploring lyrics, Orpheus sings to his audience in Hades:

> "O Gods who rule the dark and silent world,
> To you all born of a woman needs must come.
> All lovely things at last go down to you.
> You are the debtor who is always paid.
> A little while we tarry up on earth.
> Then we are yours forever and forever.
> But I seek one who came to you too soon.
> The bud was plucked before the flower bloomed.
> I tried to bear my loss. I could not bear it.
> Love was too strong a god. O King, you know
> If that old tale men tell is true, how once
> The flowers saw the rape of Proserpine.
> Then weave again for sweet Eurydice
> Life's pattern that was taken from the loom
> Too quickly. See, I ask a little thing,
> Only that you will lend, not give, her to me.
> She shall be yours when her years' span is full." (Pg. 109)

Compose a new song for Orpheus in which he beseeches the ruler of Hades to release Eurydice. The song must consist of at least ten lines; rhyming is optional.

Answers will vary.
An example song:
> *O mighty Pluto, of you I beg,*
> *To hear my lonely plea,*
> *And if this token you will grant,*
> *Your servant I shall be.*
> *My life, my soul, my love Eurydice,*
> *A maiden young and pure,*
> *Was robbed too early of her life,*
> *In this I am quite sure.*
> *To you I make this one request,*
> *Please set my lady free,*
> *So she may live her days on earth,*
> *Side by side with me.*

Activity II

Orpheus possesses a musical gift that is rivaled only by the gods, and his power has no limits when he plays and sings. The premature death of his wife, Eurydice, prompts Orpheus to travel to the underworld in an attempt to recover her. With imploring lyrics, Orpheus sings to his audience in Hades:

> "O Gods who rule the dark and silent world,
> To you all born of a woman needs must come.
> All lovely things at last go down to you.
> You are the debtor who is always paid.
> A little while we tarry up on earth.
> Then we are yours forever and forever.
> But I seek one who came to you too soon.
> The bud was plucked before the flower bloomed.
> I tried to bear my loss. I could not bear it.
> Love was too strong a god. O King, you know
> If that old tale men tell is true, how once
> The flowers saw the rape of Proserpine.
> Then weave again for sweet Eurydice
> Life's pattern that was taken from the loom
> Too quickly. See, I ask a little thing,
> Only that you will lend, not give, her to me.
> She shall be yours when her years' span is full." (Pg. 109)

Compose a new song for Orpheus in which he beseeches the ruler of Hades to release Eurydice. The song must consist of at least ten lines; rhyming is optional.

Activity III

Greek myths provide the foundation for a multitude of works of art, music, and literature. An example is the musical *My Fair Lady*, based on a play called *Pygmalion* by George Bernard Shaw, who based his work on the Greek myth of Pygmalion and Galatea. *My Fair Lady* is a story about Henry Higgins, a professor of linguistics and a confirmed bachelor, and Eliza Doolittle, a common flower girl with ambitions of becoming a proper lady. Professor Higgins takes on the challenge of transforming Miss Doolittle, whom he perceives as a lowly creature hardly worth his attention, into a gentlewoman. Eliza, in return, despises the professor because of the harsh treatment he bestows upon her. Ironically, after months of working together, a mutual appreciation and deep love forms between them.

Divide the class into groups of four. Each group should discuss and answer the following questions.

In your groups, answer the following questions:

A. Why does Pygmalion, who is a woman-hater, decide to construct a statue of a woman?

B. What reasons lead Pygmalion to fall in love with his creation?

C. Is the love Pygmalion feels for the statue Galatea complete? Why or why not?

D. Why does Venus show mercy on Pygmalion instead of seeking retribution for his earlier hatred of women?

E. Has Pygmalion's viewpoint on women as a whole changed, or is he only enamored with Galatea?

F. What similarities exist between the story of Pygmalion and Galatea and *My Fair Lady*? What are the differences?

Answers will vary.
A.   Pygmalion either cannot dismiss women from his mind or wishes to create a perfect woman in order to show men the deficiencies of their women.
B.   Pygmalion is obsessed with the perfection of his artwork.
C.   Pygmalion loves only the image of a beautiful woman and the ideal of a perfect love. He cannot appreciate the soul or personality of a statue.
D.   Venus, as the Goddess of Love, is interested in an original type of lover—a converted woman-hater.
E.   The answer to this question is largely based on opinion and speculation.
F.   The similarities are that Pygmalion and Henry Higgins are confirmed bachelors who hate women, and each man attempts to transform a woman. The differences are that Galatea is a statue who comes to life and loves Pygmalion, whereas Eliza Doolittle is a person who initially despises Henry Higgins, but eventually falls in love with him.

Activity III

Greek myths provide the foundation for a multitude of works of art, music, and literature. An example is the musical *My Fair Lady*, based on a play called *Pygmalion* by George Bernard Shaw, who based his work on the Greek myth of Pygmalion and Galatea. *My Fair Lady* is a story about Henry Higgins, a professor of linguistics and a confirmed bachelor, and Eliza Doolittle, a common flower girl with ambitions of becoming a proper lady. Professor Higgins takes on the challenge of transforming Miss Doolittle, whom he perceives as a lowly creature hardly worth his attention, into a gentlewoman. Eliza, in return, despises the professor because of the harsh treatment he bestows upon her. Ironically, after months of working together, a mutual appreciation and deep love forms between them.

In your groups, answer the following questions:

A.   Why does Pygmalion, who is a woman-hater, decide to construct a statue of a woman?

B.   What reasons lead Pygmalion to fall in love with his creation?

C.   Is the love Pygmalion feels for the statue Galatea complete? Why or why not?

D.   Why does Venus show mercy on Pygmalion instead of seeking retribution for his earlier hatred of women?

E.   Has Pygmalion's viewpoint on women as a whole changed, or is he only enamored with Galatea?

F.   What similarities exist between the story of Pygmalion and Galatea and *My Fair Lady*? What are the differences?

Group Work
Reading for Details
Tragedy
Tragic Flaw
Dialogue

Objective: Understanding the composition of a tragedy and dialogue.
                   Visualizing and depicting the details of a story.

Activity I

Euripides' *Medea*, produced in 431 B.C.E., is a tragedy based on the Greek story of Jason and Medea. In *Medea*, the contempt felt towards Jason for his treatment of Medea turns into sympathy because of Medea's horrible and deadly revenge. Medea, however, feels justified in the murder of her children because of all she has endured, and her decision is relayed in the following passage:

> "Women, my task is fixed: as quickly as I may
> To kill my children, and start away from this land,
> And not, by wasting time, to suffer my children
> To be slain by another hand less kindly to them.
> Force every way will have it they must die, and since
> This must be so, then I, their mother, shall kill them.
> O arm yourself in steel, my heart! Do not hang back
> From doing this fearful and necessary wrong.
> O come, my hand, poor wretched hand, and take the sword,
> Take it, step forward to this bitter starting point,
> And do not be a coward, do not think of them,
> How sweet they are, and how you are their mother." (from the Dover Thrift Edition of
> *Medea*, Pg. 40)

In your group, debate whether Medea's behavior is an act of mercy for her children or an act of vengeance upon Jason. Consider all the events that take place from the time Jason and Medea first meet, and decide whether or not the execution is well founded. Groups should then share their results with the rest of the class, giving the reasons for their opinions as well as backing up the reasons with evidence from the text.

> *Answers will vary.*
> *Medea is forced into assisting Jason by the gods and, as a result, she kills her brother, is alienated from her family, and exiled from her homeland. Medea travels with Jason, continuously helping him as he promises marriage and, after bearing him two sons, Medea suffers humiliation and heartbreak because of Jason's marriage to a Corinthian princess. Students must weigh all of this against the horror of Medea killing her own children.*

Group Work
Reading for Details
Tragedy
Tragic Flaw
Dialogue

Objective: Understanding the composition of a tragedy and dialogue.
Visualizing and depicting the details of a story.

Activity I

Euripides' *Medea*, produced in 431 B.C.E., is a tragedy based on the Greek story of Jason and Medea. In *Medea*, the contempt felt towards Jason for his treatment of Medea turns into sympathy because of Medea's horrible and deadly revenge. Medea, however, feels justified in the murder of her children because of all she has endured, and her decision is relayed in the following passage:

> "Women, my task is fixed: as quickly as I may
> To kill my children, and start away from this land,
> And not, by wasting time, to suffer my children
> To be slain by another hand less kindly to them.
> Force every way will have it they must die, and since
> This must be so, then I, their mother, shall kill them.
> O arm yourself in steel, my heart! Do not hang back
> From doing this fearful and necessary wrong.
> O come, my hand, poor wretched hand, and take the sword,
> Take it, step forward to this bitter starting point,
> And do not be a coward, do not think of them,
> How sweet they are, and how you are their mother." (from the Dover Thrift Edition of *Medea*, Pg. 40)

1. In your group, debate whether Medea's behavior is an act of mercy for her children or an act of vengeance upon Jason. Consider all the events that take place from the time Jason and Medea first meet, and decide whether or not the execution is well founded. Groups should then share their results with the rest of the class, giving the reasons for their opinions as well as backing up the reasons with evidence from the text.

2. Part of a tragedy centers around a main character experiencing defeat due to his or her tragic flaw. As a group, decide what tragic flaw Medea possesses, and whether or not she is defeated.

2.   Part of a tragedy centers around a main character experiencing defeat due to his or her tragic flaw. As a group, decide what tragic flaw Medea possesses, and whether or not she is defeated.

> *Answers will vary.*
> *One may argue that Medea is naïve and suffers from blind love but, at the same time, she is under the influence of Cupid's arrow. Medea is defeated in love but triumphant in vengeance. Another possible tragic flaw may be her excessive pride*

Activity II

Jason confronts Medea after learning about the death of his children, and an argument ensues about the responsibility of the deaths. Euripides writes the dialogue:

Jason:	You feel the pain yourself. You share in my sorrow.
Medea:	Yes, and my grief is gain when you cannot mock it.
Jason:	O children, what a wicked mother she was to you!
Medea:	They died from a disease they caught from their father.
Jason:	I tell you it was not my hand that destroyed them.
Medea:	But it was your insolence, and your virgin wedding.
Jason:	And just for the sake of that you chose to kill them.
Medea:	Is love so small a pain, do you think, for a woman?
Jason:	For a wise one, certainly. But you are wholly evil.
Medea:	The children are dead. I say this to make you suffer.
Jason:	The children, I think, will bring down curses on you.
Medea:	The gods know who was the author of this sorrow.
Jason:	Yes, the gods know indeed, they know your loathsome heart.

(from *Medea*, Pgs. 44-45*)*

Write a dialogue between Jason and Medea in which they confront each other about the children's deaths.

Answers will vary.
An example dialogue:

Jason:	*You monster. How could you take the lives of our children.*
Medea:	*I am the monster? It was your hand that led to this event."*
Jason:	*How can you say that when you held the knife?*
Medea:	*In helping you I have lost my family, home, and self-respect. When did I ever deny you anything?*
Jason:	*By killing my bride and children, you have denied me a happy life. You are pure evil.*
Medea:	*The gods know who is to blame. They sympathize for me, and see you as the heartless brute you truly are. Never has a human been as selfish as you. Everything that has happened is a result of your actions.*
Jason:	*I have acted only as the gods instructed me. They made you love me. I did not ask for your devotion—only your help.*

Activity II

Jason confronts Medea after learning about the death of his children, and an argument ensues about the responsibility of the deaths. Euripides writes the dialogue:

Jason: You feel the pain yourself. You share in my sorrow.

Medea: Yes, and my grief is gain when you cannot mock it.

Jason: O children, what a wicked mother she was to you!

Medea: They died from a disease they caught from their father.

Jason: I tell you it was not my hand that destroyed them.

Medea: But it was your insolence, and your virgin wedding.

Jason: And just for the sake of that you chose to kill them.

Medea: Is love so small a pain, do you think, for a woman?

Jason: For a wise one, certainly. But you are wholly evil.

Medea: The children are dead. I say this to make you suffer.

Jason: The children, I think, will bring down curses on you.

Medea: The gods know who was the author of this sorrow.

Jason: Yes, the gods know indeed, they know your loathsome heart.

(from *Medea*, Pgs. 44-45*)*

Write a dialogue between Jason and Medea in which they confront each other about the children's deaths.

Medea:	And in return, you made false promises of marriage to me. Do not think you are free of guilt.
Jason:	The only guilt is on you for the terrible deeds you have committed.
Medea:	Only the gods are my judges, not you. If I am guilty as you say, then I shall see you in Hades.

Activity III

Jason and his party encounter numerous monsters during their search for the Golden Fleece. Hamilton describes the Harpies, or the Hounds of Zeus, as "frightful flying creatures with hooked beaks and claws who always left behind them a loathsome stench." (Pg. 125) Harpies are traditionally depicted as having the head and torso of a woman, and the tail, wings, and talons of a bird. Imagine what a Harpy looks like and draw a picture of the creature or construct a collage of pictures from magazines, You may use the Internet.

Activity IV

The quest for the Golden Fleece leads Jason and the Argonauts to various lands. Retrace their journey on the following map by drawing a line of the route taken. Begin in Athens.

The starting point is Athens. From there the order of travel is the island of Lemnos, Colchis, Crete, Athens, and Corinth.

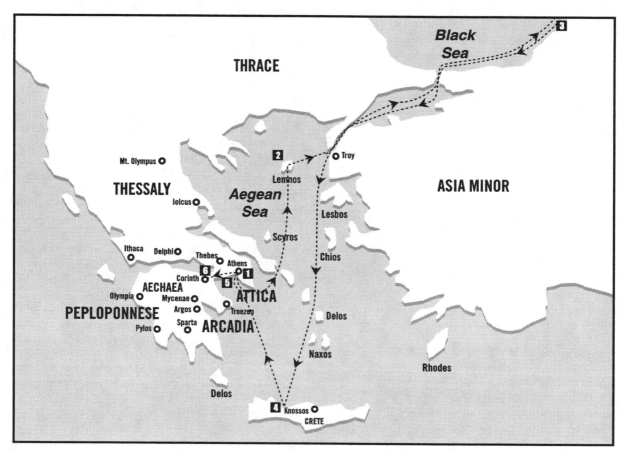

Activity III

Jason and his party encounter numerous monsters during their search for the Golden Fleece. Hamilton describes the Harpies, or the Hounds of Zeus, as "frightful flying creatures with hooked beaks and claws who always left behind them a loathsome stench." (Pg. 125) Harpies are traditionally depicted as having the head and torso of a woman, and the tail, wings, and talons of a bird. Imagine what a Harpy looks like and draw a picture of the creature or construct a collage of pictures from magazines, You may use the Internet.

Activity IV

The quest for the Golden Fleece leads Jason and the Argonauts to various lands. Retrace their journey on the following map by drawing a line of the route taken. Begin in Athens.

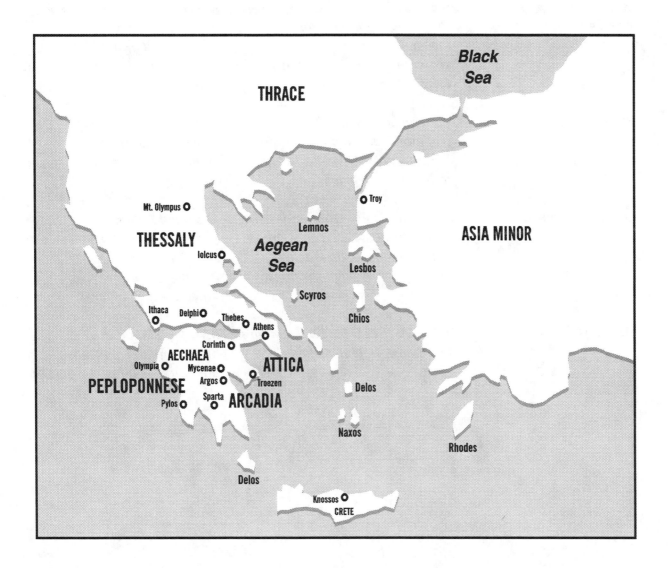

Chapter 8
Reading for Detail
Rising Action
Climax

Objective: Identifying the rising action and climax of a story.

Activity :

The rising action and climax of a story are components that keep the reader interested, and each of the four adventure stories in Chapter eight contains these elements. Complete the following chart by filling in the missing information.

Elements of Writing Chart

Story	Rising Action	Climax
Phaethon	*Phaethon looses control of the chariot, the world is set on fire, and Mother Earth cries out to Olympus.*	*Zeus throws his thunderbolt at the chariot and kills Phaethon.*
Pegasus and Bellerophon	*Bellerophon's success and ambition leads him to try to fly Pegasus up to Olympus in order to become immortal.*	*Pegasus will not fly to Olympus and throws Bellerophon from his back.*
Otus and Ephialtes	*Otus and Ephialtes, after devising a plan to capture Artemis, are in pursuit of the goddess and are chasing her through the forest.*	*Otus and Ephialtes throw their javelins, the hind disappears, and the Giants are killed by each other.*
Daedalus	*Minos devises a puzzle to capture Daedalus, which Daedalus solves.*	*Minos is slain during an attempt to capture and kill Daedalus.*

Chapter 8
Reading for Detail
Rising Action
Climax

Objective: Identifying the rising action and climax of a story.

Activity

The rising action and climax of a story are components that keep the reader interested, and each of the four adventure stories in Chapter eight contains these elements. Complete the following chart by filling in the missing information.

Elements of Writing Chart

Story	Rising Action	Climax
Phaethon		
Pegasus and Bellerophon		
Otus and Ephialtes		
Daedalus		

Chapters 9-11
Group Work

Objective: Reenacting a character's thoughts and actions.
                  Comparing heroic traits from different cultures.

Activity I

The four great Greek heroes—Perseus, Theseus, Hercules, and Atalanta—are acclaimed for their brave deeds and wondrous abilities. Their magnificent tales continue to be told today in literature, drama, and on television.

Imagine that these heroes are alive today and will be appearing on a talk show.

Choose four people from the class to each represent one of the heroes. Each person needs to be familiar with his or her hero's story to accurately answer questions. One more student will be chosen as the host, and the remainder of the class is the audience. Questions are provided to ask each hero, but the host and the audience may feel free to alter these questions or ask their own.

Answers will vary.

Perseus

1.   How do you feel about your Grandfather, King Acrisius, after he locked your mother up in the bronze underground house?

        My Grandfather acted a bit drastically, but I suppose he had a good reason—he was afraid I would be born.

2.   Why did King Acrisius set you and your mother out to sea in a box?

        He was afraid to kill us directly because the Furies would seek retribution, so he put us in the box as an almost certain way to die.

3.   Did you want to be a fisherman like Dictys or did you dream of being something else?

        I respected and loved Dictys, but I felt I could be more than just a fisherman.

4.   Why did Polydectes want to be rid of you?

        Polydectes wanted to marry my mother, but he did not want me in the bargain.

Chapters 9-11
Group Work

Objective: Reenacting a character's thoughts and actions.
Comparing heroic traits from different cultures.

Activity I

The four great Greek heroes—Perseus, Theseus, Hercules, and Atalanta—are acclaimed for their brave deeds and wondrous abilities. Their magnificent tales continue to be told today in literature, drama, and on television.

Imagine that these heroes are alive today and will be appearing on a talk show.

<u>Perseus</u>

1.   How do you feel about your Grandfather, King Acrisius, after he locked your mother up in the bronze underground house?

2.   Why did King Acrisius set you and your mother out to sea in a box?

3.   Did you want to be a fisherman like Dictys or did you dream of being something else?

4.   Why did Polydectes want to be rid of you?

5.   Why did you pledge to kill Medusa and retrieve her head?

I was the only person without an engagement gift, so I decided to get Medusa's head because Polydectes said he wanted it.

6.   How did you get the Gray Women to tell you where to find the nymphs of the North?

I stole the one eye that they all used and wouldn't return it until they answered me.

7.   What was the most resourceful weapon you had?

The helmet of invisibility, the unbreakable sword, and the bronze shield were all helpful.

8.   Who is Andromeda and why did you rescue her?

The maiden Andromeda was being sacrificed because her mother bragged of being more beautiful than the daughter of Nereus, the Sea-god. I rescued her because I fell in love with her.

9.   Why did you kill Polydectes?

He was trying to force my mother to marry him, and when she refused, he was probably going to kill her.

10.   Do you feel any guilt or remorse over the accidental death of Acrisius?

No. The Oracle foretold his death.

Theseus

1.   When were you allowed to seek your father?

As soon as I was strong enough to roll away the stone that covered the sword and shoes my father had left for me.

2.   Why did Medea try to kill you?

She did not want to lose control over my father, Aegeus.

3.   Why did you kill the Minotaur?

I wanted to end the slaughter of innocent maidens and youths.

5.   Why did you pledge to kill Medusa and retrieve her head?

6.   How did you get the Gray Women to tell you where to find the nymphs of the North?

7.   What was the most resourceful weapon you had?

8.   Who is Andromeda and why did you rescue her?

9.   Why did you kill Polydectes?

10.   Do you feel any guilt or remorse over the accidental death of Acrisius?

Theseus

1.   When were you allowed to seek your father?

2.   Why did Medea try to kill you?

3.   Why did you kill the Minotaur?

4.   What was the reason behind your father's suicide?

       He saw the black sail of my ship and thought I was dead.

5.   What do you consider the greatest deed you did for Athens?

       I created a commonwealth so that all the people were equal and could govern them-selves.

6.   Tell us how you came to be friends with Pirithous.

       Pirithous stole some of my cattle in order to challenge my heroism, but when we met, he simply shook my hand, and we became friends.

7.   Explain why there was a battle at Pirithous' wedding with the Centaurs.

       We fought because the Centaurs got drunk and tried to carry off the women.

8.   How did Pirithous die?

       He didn't die. He is sitting in the Chair of Forgetfulness in Hades.

9.   Explain the events surrounding the deaths of your wife, Phaedra, and your son, Hippolytus.

       Hippolytus scorned Aphrodite because she represented everything soft and feminine and, as a means of revenge, Aphrodite made Phaedra fall in love with Hippolytus. When her love was scorned, Pheadra killed herself and left a note saying Hippolytus had raped her, which was untrue. I banished my son before finding out the truth and, upon leaving home, he was mortally wounded by a sea monster.

Hercules

1.   How did you get into an argument with Apollo?

       His oracle wouldn't answer my question, so I threatened to carry her off unless I got a response.

2.   Who was the first person you killed?

       As a boy, I brained my music teacher with his lute.

4.   What was the reason behind your father's suicide?

5.   What do you consider the greatest deed you did for Athens?

6.   Tell us how you came to be friends with Pirithous.

7.   Explain why there was a battle at Pirithous' wedding with the Centaurs.

8.   How did Pirithous die?

9.   Explain the events surrounding the deaths of your wife, Phaedra, and your son, Hippolytus.

Hercules

1.   How did you get into an argument with Apollo?

2.   Who was the first person you killed?

3.   Explain the circumstances surrounding the deaths of your wife and children.

Hera made me temporarily mad, and I killed them while out of my mind and completely unaware of my actions.

4.   Why didn't you kill yourself after the tragic death of your family?

Theseus grasped my bloodied hands, thus sharing in the guilt of the deaths, and he convinced me to stay alive and be strong.

5.   What was the purpose of the twelve tasks you completed for Eurystheus? Which task proved the most difficult?

The tasks were intended to purify me for the murder of my family. The last task, retrieving the three-headed dog Cerberus from Hades, proved the most difficult.

6.   How did you come to wed Deianira, your second wife?

I fought the river god Achelous while he was in the shape of a bull and broke off one of his horns.

7.   Why did you travel to Hades and retrieve Queen Alcestis?

I got obnoxiously drunk while visiting Admetus, unaware that he was mourning the death of his wife. To make amends, I rescued her from death.

8.   How did Deianira die?

She became jealous and tried to poison me. When the poison didn't kill me, she killed herself.

9.   Were you and Hera ever reconciled?

After I died, Hera and I made peace, and I married her daughter.

Atalanta

1.   Why did your father abandon you on a mountainside when you were an infant?

He was bitterly disappointed that I wasn't a boy.

2.   After you assisted Meleager with killing the Calydonian boar, he insisted you keep the skin. Do you feel you deserved it?

I think I deserved the skin because I made the first wound.

3. Explain the circumstances surrounding the deaths of your wife and children.

4. Why didn't you kill yourself after the tragic death of your family?

5. What was the purpose of the twelve tasks you completed for Eurystheus? Which task proved the most difficult?

6. How did you come to wed Deianira, your second wife?

7. Why did you travel to Hades and retrieve Queen Alcestis?

8. How did Deianira die?

9. Were you and Hera ever reconciled?

Atalanta

1. Why did your father abandon you on a mountainside when you were an infant?

2. After you assisted Meleager with killing the Calydonian boar, he insisted you keep the skin. Do you feel you deserved it?

3.   How did Meleager die, and do you blame yourself for his death?

Meleager got into an argument with his uncles about giving me the boar skin and, as a result, he killed them. His mother, upset about the deaths of her brothers, killed Meleager with a magical log. Meleager's fate was to stay alive as long as the log was not burned.
No, I do not blame myself for his death. I blame his mother.

4.   How did you rediscover your parents?

My parents were discovered when I wrestled Peleus at the funeral games for Pelias.

5.   What measures did you take to keep from marrying anyone?

I agreed to marry anyone who could beat me in a foot race, knowing that no one could.

6.   How did Melanion beat you in the race?

He had three irresistible, gold apples, and threw each apple off the track in order to distract me from the race.

3.   How did Meleager die, and do you blame yourself for his death?

4.   How did you rediscover your parents?

5.   What measures did you take to keep from marrying anyone?

6.   How did Melanion beat you in the race?

Chapters 13-14
Character Comprehension

Objective: Identifying the essential characters and events of the Trojan War.

The beginning of Greek literature is marked by *The Iliad*, which cannot be accurately dated, and which is attributed to the poet Homer, about whom nothing is known except his name. *The Iliad* describes the events of a few weeks in the ten-year siege of Troy. The particular subject of the epic poem is the anger of Achilles; the crisis of the poem is the duel between Achilles and Hector. War and peace, with their corresponding aspects of human nature are implicit in every situation and statement of the poem.

Activity I

A. The story of the Trojan War is a complicated tale full of numerous characters. Match the following descriptions to the appropriate characters.

Character		Description
1. Patroclus	_____	A. Queen of Troy
2. Achilles	_____	B. Fairest woman in the world; cause of Trojan War
3. Hecuba	_____	C. Achilles' best friend; killed by Hector
4. Odysseus	_____	D. Husband chosen for Helen; King of Sparta
5. Pandarus	_____	E. Nymph abandoned by Paris
6. Paris	_____	F. King of Troy
7. Oenone	_____	G. Achilles' mother
8. Andromache	_____	H. Evil goddess of Discord
9. Agamemnon	_____	I. Greatest Greek warrior and victor; weakness in the heel
10. Eris	_____	J. His judgment began the Trojan War
11. Briseis	_____	K. King of Ithaca; feigned madness to avoid going to war
12. Thetis	_____	L. Broke truce by shooting an arrow at Menelaus
13. Priam	_____	M. Maiden who was stolen from Achilles
14. Helen	_____	N. Hector's wife
15. Hector	_____	O. Greek commander who steals Achilles' prize of honor
16. Menelaus	_____	P. Prince of Troy; "Tamer of Horses;" lost to Achilles

Answer Key

1. C	5. L	9. O	13. F
2. I	6. J	10. H	14. B
3. A	7. E	11. M	15. P
4. K	8. N	12. G	16. D

Chapters 13-14
Character Comprehension

Objective: Identifying the essential characters and events of the Trojan War.

The beginning of Greek literature is marked by *The Iliad*, which cannot be accurately dated, and which is attributed to the poet Homer, about whom nothing is known except his name. *The Iliad* describes the events of a few weeks in the ten-year siege of Troy. The particular subject of the epic poem is the anger of Achilles; the crisis of the poem is the duel between Achilles and Hector. War and peace, with their corresponding aspects of human nature are implicit in every situation and statement of the poem.

Activity I

A. The story of the Trojan War is a complicated tale full of numerous characters. Match the following descriptions to the appropriate characters.

Character		Description
1. Patroclus	_____	A. Queen of Troy
2. Achilles	_____	B. Fairest woman in the world; cause of Trojan War
3. Hecuba	_____	C. Achilles' best friend; killed by Hector
4. Odysseus	_____	D. Husband chosen for Helen; King of Sparta
5. Pandarus	_____	E. Nymph abandoned by Paris
6. Paris	_____	F. King of Troy
7. Oenone	_____	G. Achilles' mother
8. Andromache	_____	H. Evil goddess of Discord
9. Agamemnon	_____	I. Greatest Greek warrior and victor; weakness in the heel
10. Eris	_____	J. His judgment began the Trojan War
11. Briseis	_____	K. King of Ithaca; feigned madness to avoid going to war
12. Thetis	_____	L. Broke truce by shooting an arrow at Menelaus
13. Priam	_____	M. Maiden who was stolen from Achilles
14. Helen	_____	N. Hector's wife
15. Hector	_____	O. Greek commander who steals Achilles' prize of honor
16. Menelaus	_____	P. Prince of Troy; "Tamer of Horses;" lost to Achilles

B. As the Trojan War raged on between the Greeks and Trojans, the gods each chose a favorite side. A list of gods is provided below. Place each god under the appropriate column in the chart below, according to which side he or she supported.

Hera	Apollo
Zeus	Poseidon
Athena	Artemis
Ares	Aphrodite

Greek	**Trojan**
Hera	*Aphrodite*
Athena	*Ares*
Poseidon	*Apollo*
	Artemis
	Zeus

B. As the Trojan War raged on between the Greeks and Trojans, the gods each chose a favorite side. A list of gods is provided below. Place each god under the appropriate column in the chart below, according to which side he or she supported.

Hera	Apollo
Zeus	Poseidon
Athena	Artemis
Ares	Aphrodite

Greek	Trojan

Activity II

Note to Teacher: Students may need to use the newspaper appendix for these activities.

You are a journalist for the New York Times, and your boss has instructed you to cover the story of the destruction of Troy. Starting with the death of Hector, write an article describing the events leading to the fall of the city. Be sure to title your article and, if you like, include any comments made by witnesses.

Answers will vary.
A sample article:

Ten-Year Siege Comes to a Close

The ten-year long war between Greece and the city of Troy finally came to an end Sunday with the fall of Troy.

Even after the death of Hector, the great Trojan warrior, the Greeks continued to be hard pressed as Trojan allies arrived from Ethiopia. The tides changed, however, with the death of Memnon, the Ethiopian Prince, at the hands of Achilles, the Greek champion. Achilles' death followed shortly thereafter when he received an arrow in the heel from Paris.

With their great leader gone, the Greeks now followed the rule of Odysseus, whose ingenuity led to the final stages of the war. After constructing a large wooden horse, a select few leaders, including Odysseus, hid within the stomach while the remaining Greek army retreated to a nearby island. The Trojans, finding the Greek camp abandoned, believed the Greeks had departed for home.

Only one man, Sinon, had been left behind. He convinced the Trojans that the Greeks had intended to sacrifice him but that he had escaped. Sinon also explained to the Trojans that the large horse had been built as an homage to Athena, and should they take it within their walls, the goddess would be appeased. Without hesitation, the Trojans wheeled the monument inside their city walls.

That night the door of the horse opened and one by one the chieftains let themselves out. Throwing the city gates open, the Greek army rushed in and took the sleeping city by surprise. It was a slaughter. By morning the once-proud city was a fiery ruin.

The few survivors consisted of women and children, who were immediately separated and shipped to Greece to be sold as slaves. Thus ends the Trojan War.

Activity III

Write an editorial that deals with the beginnings of the Trojan War. Write a headline for this editorial and make sure you back it up with facts from the story.

Activity II

You are a journalist for the New York Times, and your boss has instructed you to cover the story of the destruction of Troy. Starting with the death of Hector, write an article describing the events leading to the fall of the city. Be sure to title your article and, if you like, include any comments made by witnesses.

Activity III

Write an editorial that deals with the beginnings of the Trojan War. Write a headline for this editorial and make sure you back it up with facts from the story.

Chapter 15
Creative Writing
Character Comparison
Epic Hero

Objective: Developing writing skills through creative revision.

Activity :

The Odyssey is a Homeric epic pertaining to the long, drawn-out return home of Odysseus of Ithaca, who spent ten years wandering throughout the world. Odysseus struggles for life, and his outstanding quality is a probing and versatile intelligence that, combined with long experience, keeps him safe and alive. The adventures on the voyage home test Odysseus' mental and physical abilities and, throughout the journey, he manages to preserve the heroic reputation that he won in the Trojan War. In Homer's *The Odyssey*, Odysseus gives Penelope an account of his adventures:

> He began with the Ciconian battles, and went on to the Lotus-eaters' country, and what the Cyclops is, and how he avenged those fine fellows whom the cannibal devoured without pity; the visit of Aiolos, how kindly he had received them and helped them on their voyage; but it was not yet his destiny to reach home–the tempest caught him up again, and drove him over the sea in distress. Then how he cam to Laisrygonian Telepylos, and the natives destroyed the ships and their crews. He told of Circe's tricks and devices, and how he sailed to the mouldering house of Hades to consult the soul of Theban Teiresias; how he saw his old comrades, and the mother who had bone him and brought him up; how he heard the throbbing notes of Sirens' song; how he went on to the Moving Rocks, and dread Charybdis, and Scylla, whom no man ever escaped unharmed; how his companions slaughtered the Sun's cattle; how Zeus thundering in the heights struck the ship with a fiery bolt, and his companions were destroyed every one; how he alone escaped, and came to Ogygia and the nymph Calypso; how she kept him in her cave and wanted to have him for a husband, how she cared for him and promised to make him immortal, never to grow old, but he would never consent; how after great hardships he reached the Phaiacians, and they treated him with right royal kindness and conveyed him to Ithaca in one of their ships, with a heap of gifts, bronze and gold and fine woven stuffs. (from the W.H.D. Rouse translation of *The Odyssey*, Pg. 259)

Chapter 15
Creative Writing
Character Comparison
Epic Hero

Objective: Developing writing skills through creative revision.

Activity

The Odyssey is a Homeric epic pertaining to the long, drawn-out return home of Odysseus of Ithaca, who spent ten years wandering throughout the world. Odysseus struggles for life, and his outstanding quality is a probing and versatile intelligence that, combined with long experience, keeps him safe and alive. The adventures on the voyage home test Odysseus' mental and physical abilities and, throughout the journey, he manages to preserve the heroic reputation that he won in the Trojan War. In Homer's *The Odyssey*, Odysseus gives Penelope an account of his adventures:

> He began with the Ciconian battles, and went on to the Lotus-eaters' country, and what the Cyclops is, and how he avenged those fine fellows whom the cannibal devoured without pity; the visit of Aiolos, how kindly he had received them and helped them on their voyage; but it was not yet his destiny to reach home–the tempest caught him up again, and drove him over the sea in distress. Then how he cam to Laisrygonian Telepylos, and the natives destroyed the ships and their crews. He told of Circe's tricks and devices, and how he sailed to the mouldering house of Hades to consult the soul of Theban Teiresias; how he saw his old comrades, and the mother who had bone him and brought him up; how he heard the throbbing notes of Sirens' song; how he went on to the Moving Rocks, and dread Charybdis, and Scylla, whom no man ever escaped unharmed; how his companions slaughtered the Sun's cattle; how Zeus thundering in the heights struck the ship with a fiery bolt, and his companions were destroyed every one; how he alone escaped, and came to Ogygia and the nymph Calypso; how she kept him in her cave and wanted to have him for a husband, how she cared for him and promised to make him immortal, never to grow old, but he would never consent; how after great hardships he reached the Phaiacians, and they treated him with right royal kindness and conveyed him to Ithaca in one of their ships, with a heap of gifts, bronze and gold and fine woven stuffs. (from the W.H.D. Rouse translation of *The Odyssey*, Pg. 259)

Activity II

Just as Odysseus is a hero of ancient Greece, Beowulf is an Anglo-Saxon, Christian hero. Read the following synopsis on Beowulf and complete the comparison chart so that you can see similarities among the main characters.

> *Beowulf*, composed about 850 C.E., in England, is a heroic poem of dark magnificence and a vivid account of the social world of the Germanic and Scandinavian people. The hero Beowulf, a Geat from the court of King Hygelac, travels to the court of Hrothgar in Denmark to kill the monster Grendel. Grendel is an evil spirit condemned for being a descendent of Cain, whom God punished for slaying his brother, Abel. For twelve years, the monster plundered Hrothgar's great hall and murdered the people.
>
> A large banquet is held upon the arrival of Beowulf and his men, and afterwards the warriors retire in the great hall. That night Grendel arrives. Creeping out of the shadows, Grendel manages to kill a man before Beowulf fearlessly grabs a hold of him and cuts off his hand. Terrified and mortally wounded, Grendel flees from the hall to seek his dying-place.
>
> Grendel's mother, determined to seek vengeance for her son's death, sneaks into the great hall, kills a man, and runs away. Beowulf advises the Danish king, "It is better for a man to avenge his friend than much mourn." Beowulf travels to the bottom of the lake where Grendel's mother lives, fighting cold currents and sea-beasts along the way. A fierce battle ensues, much of which is hand-to-hand combat, and Beowulf triumphs with a deadly thrust of his sword. Beowulf triumphantly returns to his homeland and eventually becomes king.
>
> Fifty years later, when Beowulf is an old man, a dragon begins to menace the land. Beowulf bravely fights and slays the dragon, but he is mortally wounded during the battle. A great funeral pyre is built and Beowulf receives a hero's burial. Beowulf is recognized as worthy not because he is thoughtful or self-controlled (although he is both) but because he is fierce in battle.

Activity II

Just as Odysseus is a hero of ancient Greece, Beowulf is an Anglo-Saxon, Christian hero. Read the following synopsis on Beowulf and complete the comparison chart so that you can see similarities among the main characters.

Beowulf, composed about 850 C.E., in England, is a heroic poem of dark magnificence and a vivid account of the social world of the Germanic and Scandinavian people. The hero Beowulf, a Geat from the court of King Hygelac, travels to the court of Hrothgar in Denmark to kill the monster Grendel. Grendel is an evil spirit condemned for being a descendent of Cain, whom God punished for slaying his brother, Abel. For twelve years, the monster plundered Hrothgar's great hall and murdered the people.

A large banquet is held upon the arrival of Beowulf and his men, and afterwards the warriors retire in the great hall. That night Grendel arrives. Creeping out of the shadows, Grendel manages to kill a man before Beowulf fearlessly grabs a hold of him and cuts off his hand. Terrified and mortally wounded, Grendel flees from the hall to seek his dying-place.

Grendel's mother, determined to seek vengeance for her son's death, sneaks into the great hall, kills a man, and runs away. Beowulf advises the Danish king, "It is better for a man to avenge his friend than much mourn." Beowulf travels to the bottom of the lake where Grendel's mother lives, fighting cold currents and sea-beasts along the way. A fierce battle ensues, much of which is hand-to-hand combat, and Beowulf triumphs with a deadly thrust of his sword. Beowulf triumphantly returns to his homeland and eventually becomes king.

Fifty years later, when Beowulf is an old man, a dragon begins to menace the land. Beowulf bravely fights and slays the dragon, but he is mortally wounded during the battle. A great funeral pyre is built and Beowulf receives a hero's burial. Beowulf is recognized as worthy not because he is thoughtful or self-controlled (although he is both) but because he is fierce in battle.

Hero Comparison Chart

Question *Answers may vary.*	Odysseus	Beowulf
For what reason does the hero fight monsters?	*personal survival*	*to aid another kingdom*
How is religion a part of the story?	*the gods interfere with his life*	*the monsters are descendants of Cain*
How does this person fit the definition of an epic hero?	*bravery; conquers problems*	*bravery; overcomes evil with good*
How does the civilization view a classic hero?	*strong and cunning*	*strong and fearless*
What is the hero's most helpful fighting tool?	*brain*	*sword*
How does he die?	*The excerpt does not say. (Odysseus, however, was killed by the son he had, but never saw, with Circe.)*	*In battle with a monster*

Activity III

An epitaph is an inscription, such as on a tombstone, in memory of a deceased person. The writing can briefly describe the person's strong traits and what he or she will be remembered for. Write an epitaph for both Odysseus and Beowulf, summarizing their life accomplishments or positive qualities.

Answers will vary.
Example of epitaph:
Here lies Odysseus, a loving husband and father, Greek warrior, and great adventurer.
Beowulf: king, hero, defender of right.

Question	Odysseus	Beowulf
For what reason does the hero fight monsters?		
How is religion a part of the story?		
How does this person fit the definition of an epic hero?		
How does the civilization view a classic hero?		
What is the hero's most helpful fighting tool?		
How does he die?		

Activity III

An epitaph is an inscription, such as on a tombstone, in memory of a deceased person. The writing can briefly describe the person's strong traits and what he or she will be remembered for. Write an epitaph for both Odysseus and Beowulf, summarizing their life accomplishments or positive qualities.

Chapters 1-26
Epithets
Image

Throughout this book, Edith Hamilton refers to people and gods through the use of epithets. For example: "implacable Charybdis," and "Aeolus, the King of the Winds." List each epithet you can find in the blank next to the name. Across from each one, write the image that is suggested by the word or phrase. We have done the first one for you as an example.

Implacable Charybdis (Pg. 232)

It implies that even as Charybdis' whirlpool pulled ships under the water, the monster did not care.

Many ridged Olympus (Pg.25)

Golden-throned Hera (Pg. 28)

Poseidon *Earth-shaker* (Pg. 29)

black-winged Night (Pg. 65)

Earth *the beautiful* (Pg. 66)

Hercules, *greatest of heroes* (Pg. 81)

Odysseus, *wrecker of cities* (Pg. 88)

Harpies, *hounds of Zeus* (Pg. 125)

Throughout this book, Edith Hamilton refers to people and gods through the use of epithets. For example: "implacable Charybdis," and "Aeolus, the King of the Winds." List each epithet you can find in the blank next to the name. Across from each one, write the image that is suggested by the word or phrase. We have done the first one for you as an example.

Implacable Charybdis (Pg. 232)

It implies that even as Charybdis' whirlpool pulled ships under the water, the monster did not care.

_____Olympus (Pg.25)

_____Hera (Pg. 28)

Poseidon _____(Pg. 29)

_____Night (Pg. 65)

Earth _____(Pg. 66)

Hercules, _____(Pg. 81)

Odysseus, _____(Pg. 88)

Harpies, _____(Pg. 125)

evil goddess of discord Eris (Pg. 186)

silver-footed Thetis (Pg. 191)

fleet-footed Antilochus (Pg. 197)

Hector, *tamer of horses* (Pg. 200)

Hecate, *the dread Goddess of Night* (Pg. 237)

death-dealing War (Pg. 237)

mad Discord (Pg. 237)

_____Eris (Pg. 186)

_____Thetis (Pg. 191)

_____Antilochus (Pg. 197)

Hector, _____(Pg. 200)

Hecate, _____(Pg. 237)

_____War (Pg. 237)

_____Discord (Pg. 237)

Activity II

Make up an epithet for the following and explain how the epithet describes the noun. We have done the first one for you. You may place the epithet before or after the name, and you may eliminate the person's first name if it sounds better.

sharp-clawed eagle   This implies that the eagle's claws are its most
                                                  effective weapon.

George Washington

cheetah

Michael Jackson

Grand Canyon

Abe Lincoln

Dracula

Muhammad Ali

Adolph Hitler

the moon

Activity II

Make up an epithet for the following and explain how the epithet describes the noun. We have done the first one for you. You may place the epithet before or after the name, and you may eliminate the person's first name if it sounds better.

sharp-clawed eagle   This implies that the eagle's claws are its most effective weapon.

George Washington

cheetah

Michael Jackson

Grand Canyon

Abe Lincoln

Dracula

Muhammad Ali

Adolph Hitler

the moon

New York City

Cadillac

Homer Simpson

Moby Dick

Genghis Khan

New York City

Cadillac

Homer Simpson

Moby Dick

Genghis Khan

Chapter 27
Reading for Details
Creative Writing
Deus ex Machina

Objective: Charting the family lineage of the House of Atreus.
                   Using deus ex machina to complete stories.

Activity I

The members of the House of Atreus are deeply imbedded in Greek mythology. Using the information in chapter seventeen, complete the following family tree by filling in the missing names.

House of Atreus

Tantalus

Amphion   marries   *Niobe*   *Pelops*   marries   *Hippodamia*

14 Children

Atreus   *Thyestes*

Aegisthus   *Pittheus*

Helen   marries   *Menelaus*   *Agamemnon* marries *Clytemnestra*

Iphigenia   *Orestes*   *Electra*

Chapter 27
Reading for Details
Creative Writing
Deus ex Machina

Objective: Charting the family lineage of the House of Atreus.
Using deus ex machina to complete stories.

Activity I

The members of the House of Atreus are deeply imbedded in Greek mythology. Using the information in chapter seventeen, complete the following family tree by filling in the missing names.

House of Atreus

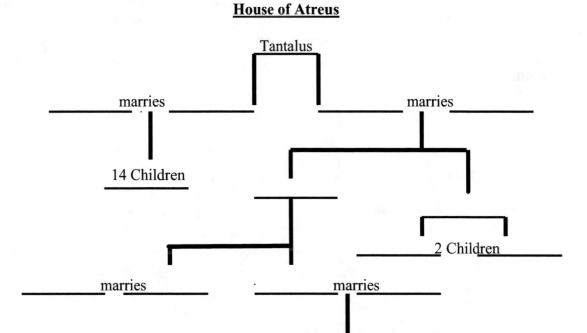

Activity II

The story of Iphigenia's escape from the Taurians is a perfect example of deus ex machina. Escape is impossible, and death is inevitable for Iphigenia and her companions until Athena intervenes.

Rewrite the ending of Iphigenia's story after Orestes' ship is stopped by the wind. Show what would happen if Athena had not intervened in the escape.

Answers will vary. An example ending:
Unable to pass through the mouth of the harbor, they were forced to land on the shore. King Thoas, angry about the attempted escape, dispatched soldiers to arrest Iphigenia, Orestes, and Pylades. In the palace, King Thoas pardoned Iphigenia out of fear of Artemis' wrath for killing a priestess, but he sentenced Orestes and Pylades to immediate death. Iphigenia refused to watch her family slain. She told Thoas that Orestes was her brother and Pylades her cousin, and if he killed her family then she, as Artemis' priestess, would have the goddess destroy the kingdom. Fearful of the goddess's wrath, King Thoas released his prisoners. They once again boarded their ship and departed, and this time the winds were calm.

Probing further:

List one book, movie, or television show that you have encountered that makes of deus ex machina.

Answers may vary. Example:

Superman was nearly dead from Kryptonite poisoning, but an earthquake occurred, and the Kryptonite fell into a crack, away from him.

Activity II

The story of Iphigenia's escape from the Taurians is a perfect example of deus ex machina. Escape is impossible, and death is inevitable for Iphigenia and her companions until Athena intervenes.

Rewrite the ending of Iphigenia's story after Orestes' ship is stopped by the wind. Show what would happen if Athena had not intervened in the escape.

Probing further:

List one book, movie, or television show that you have encountered that makes of deus ex machina.

Chapter 18
Reading Comprehension
Irony
Tragic Flaw

Objective: Recognizing irony in *Oedipus the King*.

Activity I

Oedipus is a man with high principles and probing intelligence who follows the prompting of that intelligence to the final consequence of true self-knowledge. He learns that the prophecy he had first fought against and then laughed at has been fulfilled, that every step he took was one step closer to disaster, and that he could not fight his fate.

Note to teacher: This activity is aimed at students who are proficient at character analysis.

Based upon Oedipus' story, answer the following questions.

1.   What irony can be found in the story?

   Oedipus leaves Corinth to avoid killing his supposed father, Polybus, and ends up killing his actual father, Laius, on the road. Oedipus undergoes a relentless search for the murderer of Laius when he himself is the person responsible. Oedipus has strong moral principles, but, despite them, he kills his father and marries his mother out of ignorance.

2.   What is Oedipus' tragic flaw?

   Oedipus uses his intelligence to outsmart the oracle and the Sphinx, but in the end he outsmarts himself.

3.   Explain the symbolism of Oedipus blinding himself.

   Oedipus failed to see the truth of his origin and life until it was too late. Reality was too awful to face, so he blinded himself to escape.

4.   Just as with Oedipus, irony is found in the story of his children. Explain the irony in the events surrounding the deaths of Ismene and Polyneices.

   Polyneices receives proper burial only at the cost of Ismene's death.

Chapter 18
Reading Comprehension
Irony
Tragic Flaw

Objective: Recognizing irony in *Oedipus the King*.

Activity I

Oedipus is a man with high principles and probing intelligence who follows the prompting of that intelligence to the final consequence of true self-knowledge. He learns that the prophecy he had first fought against and then laughed at has been fulfilled, that every step he took was one step closer to disaster, and that he could not fight his fate.

Based upon Oedipus' story, answer the following questions.

1.   What irony can be found in the story?

2.   What is Oedipus' tragic flaw?

3.   Explain the symbolism of Oedipus blinding himself.

4.   Just as with Oedipus, irony is found in the story of his children. Explain the irony in the events surrounding the deaths of Ismene and Polyneices.

Chapter 19
Visualization
Characterization
Inference

Objective: Inferring the thoughts and feelings of a character.

Activity II

Suppose the media hears about the story of Creusa and a reporter is dispatched to interview her. Based on the information in the book, answer the questions in the interview as if you were Creusa.

Answers will vary.
The activity may be performed as role-playing or as a written activity.

Reporter: Your contempt for Apollo was well known. Did you at any time ever fear his anger?

Creusa: *No, not after he attacked me. My life was already ruined, so I didn't care.*

Reporter: Why did you hide your child from your family? Didn't you think they would be happy that a god chose you? What would they have done if they had known?

Creusa: *Our society frowns at an unmarried woman having a child. I knew it didn't matter whether or not the father was a god; it would have been unforgivable. I would have been outcast or even killed.*

Reporter: How did you feel about leaving your son in the cave? What did you expect to find when you returned?

Creusa: *It was difficult to abandon my son in the cave because I knew he would die. When I returned to the cave I thought he would be dead, and I was shocked to find him missing without a trace.*

Reporter: What were your feelings about marrying Xuthus, a foreigner to Athens? Were you upset that you couldn't have any children?

Creusa: *I knew people looked down upon my husband for being an outsider, but I had to follow the wishes of my father. I was grateful that Xuthus had helped my father in the past. It bothered me a little that I could not have any more children, but I assumed it was the work of Apollo.*

Objective: Inferring the thoughts and feelings of a character.

Activity II

Suppose the media hears about the story of Creusa and a reporter is dispatched to interview her. Based on the information in the book, answer the questions in the interview as if you were Creusa.

Reporter: Your contempt for Apollo was well known. Did you at any time ever fear his anger?

Creusa:

Reporter: Why did you hide your child from your family? Didn't you think they would be happy that a god chose you? What would they have done if they had known?

Creusa:

Reporter: How did you feel about leaving your son in the cave? What did you expect to find when you returned?

Creusa:

Reporter: What were your feelings about marrying Xuthus, a foreigner to Athens?
Were you upset that you couldn't have any children?

Creusa:

Reporter: Upon arriving at the temple in Delphi and talking with Ion, your resolve of facing Apollo weakened. Why did you begin to change your mind?

Creusa: *Ion convinced me it was not a good idea to anger the god with accusations.*

Reporter: Why weren't you happy at first when Ion was given to you as a son?

Creusa: *I didn't want an unknown person's abandoned son.*

Reporter: How did you feel when you discovered Ion was your real son?

Creusa: *I was relieved he was alive and happy to be reunited. The years I suffered had finally come to an end.*

Reporter: Upon arriving at the temple in Delphi and talking with Ion, your resolve of facing Apollo weakened. Why did you begin to change your mind?

Creusa:

Reporter: Why weren't you happy at first when Ion was given to you as a son?

Creusa:

Reporter: How did you feel when you discovered Ion was your real son?

Creusa:

Chapters 17-19
Group Work
Oratory

Objective: Assessing the great families of mythology to determine which is the most tragic lineage.

Activity I

Divide the class into small groups of three or four students.
Each group must evaluate the great families of Greek mythology—Atreus, Thebes, and Athens—to decide which has the most tragic history. A second choice for a speech is to determine which one of the families is least or most responsible for its own fate. Compose a convincing speech by using information from the text to support your conclusion. The group will then assign a speaker to present the speech to the class.

Answers will vary.

Chapters 17-19
Group Work
Oratory

Objective: Assessing the great families of mythology to determine which is the most tragic lineage.

Activity I

Each group must evaluate the great families of Greek mythology—Atreus, Thebes, and Athens—to decide which has the most tragic history. A second choice for a speech is to determine which one of the families is least or most responsible for its own fate. Compose a convincing speech by using information from the text to support your conclusion. The group will then assign a speaker to present the speech to the class.

Chapter 20
Simile
Metaphor
Anecdote

Objective: Expressing suggestive communication.

Activity I

Rewrite each of the following statements by using both a simile and a metaphor. Don't worry about using all the words from the statement. The goal is to create clear and vivid communication.

Answers may vary.

1.   Midas can turn things into gold.

Simile	*Metaphor*
Midas is a walking gold mine.	*Midas wants gold like a man in the desert wants water*

2.   Aesculapius is a great physician.

Aesculapius is like a miracle worker.

3.   The Danaids kill their husbands.

The Danaids are like black widow spiders.

4.   Circe is jealous of Glaucus' love for Scylla.

Circe is a green-eyed monster.

5.   Erysichthon never stops eating.

Erysichthon's stomach is a bottomless pit.

6.   Erysichthon's daughter continuously changes shape.

The daughter's shape changes like the wind.

Chapter 20
Simile
Metaphor
Anecdote

Objective: Expressing suggestive communication.

Activity I

Rewrite each of the following statements by using both a simile and a metaphor. Don't worry about using all the words from the statement. The goal is to create clear and vivid communication.

1.   Midas can turn things into gold.

2.   Aesculapius is a great physician.

3.   The Danaids kill their husbands.

4.   Circe is jealous of Glaucus' love for Scylla.

5.   Erysichthon never stops eating.

6.   Erysichthon's daughter continuously changes shape.

Activity II

The story of Midas depicts the consequences of his thoughtless acts. Hamilton writes:

> "He was an example of folly being as fatal as sin, for he meant no harm; he merely did not use any intelligence." (Pg. 292)

Compose an anecdote about Midas in which he still possesses his gift of the golden touch. Be sure to display in your story the careless and often stupid behavior of the King.

Answers will vary.

Activity II

The story of Midas depicts the consequences of his thoughtless acts. Hamilton writes:

> "He was an example of folly being as fatal as sin, for he meant no harm; he merely did not use any intelligence." (Pg. 292)

Compose an anecdote about Midas in which he still possesses his gift of the golden touch. Be sure to display in your story the careless and often stupid behavior of the King.

Chapter 21
Character Comprehension

Objective: Becoming familiar with minor mythological characters.

Activity I

Various myths are briefly introduced in this chapter. Complete the crossword puzzle in order to become more familiar with the characters.

Chapter 21
Character Comprehension

Objective: Becoming familiar with minor mythological characters.

Activity I

Various myths are briefly introduced in this chapter. Complete the crossword puzzle in order to become more familiar with the characters.

Across

1	Slept for fifty-seven years
4	Seven sisters; the rainy stars
10	Immortal husband of Aurora
14	Men created from ants
15	Daughters of Atlas; pursued by Orion
18	Great Bear constellation
19	Kind Centaur; killed by Hercules
20	He understood all flying and creeping creatures
21	Died while impersonating Zeus

Down

2	Lost to Apollo in flute contest
3	Changed into a spider by Minerva
5	Lesser Bear constellation
6	Theban princess; Bore Zeus two sons
7	Torn to pieces by dogs as a youth
8	Changed into a sunflower
9	Changed into a tree for plucking a blossom
11	Poet saved by dolphins
12	Forever rolling a rock uphill in Hades
13	Keeper of bees
16	Nation of female warriors
17	Constellation; huntsman of Artemis

Answer key

Across
1. *Epimenides*
4. *Hyades*
10. *Tithonus*
14. *Myrmidons*
15. *Pleiades*
18. *Callisto*
19. *Chiron*
20. *Melampus*
21. *Salmoneus*

Down
2. *Marsyas*
3. *Arachne*
5. *Areas*
6. *Antiope*
7. *Linus*
8. *Clytie*
9. *Dryope*
11. *Arion*
12. *Sisyphus*
13. *Aristaeus*
16. *Amazons*
17. *Orion*

Across

1	Slept for fifty-seven years
4	Seven sisters; the rainy stars
10	Immortal husband of Aurora
14	Men created from ants
15	Daughters of Atlas; pursued by Orion
18	Great Bear constellation
19	Kind Centaur; killed by Hercules
20	He understood all flying and creeping creatures
21	Died while impersonating Zeus

Down

2	Lost to Apollo in flute contest
3	Changed into a spider by Minerva
5	Lesser Bear constellation
6	Theban princess; Bore Zeus two sons
7	Torn to pieces by dogs as a youth
8	Changed into a sunflower
9	Changed into a tree for plucking a blossom
11	Poet saved by dolphins
12	Forever rolling a rock uphill in Hades
13	Keeper of bees
16	Nation of female warriors
17	Constellation; huntsman of Artemis

Chapter 22
Group Work
Character Comparison
Oral Tradition

Objective: Weighing the traits of Greek and Norse characters.
Enacting oral tradition through a revision and continuation of a myth.

Activity I

The tragic story of Signy shares similar traits with the story of Clytemnestra, as told in chapter seventeen. Complete the comparison chart in order to attain a better understanding of the similarities and differences between the two women.

Comparison Chart

Question	Clytemnestra	Signy
What is the motive for revenge?	*death of daughter*	*death of father and brothers*
Who is the target of revenge?	*husband*	*husband and children*
How long did she wait to be avenged?	*ten years*	*until her son became a man*
Did she have an accomplice? If so, who?	*yes—Aegisthus*	*yes—Sigmund and Sinfiotli*
Is the revenge satisfying?	*yes*	*yes*
How did she die?	*Orestes killed her*	*committed suicide*
Do you think her revenge was justified or unjustified?	*answers will vary*	*answers will vary*
How does she depict the women of her culture (Greek and Norse)?	*answers will vary* *patient, passionate*	*answers will vary* *strong-willed, patient*

Chapter 22
Group Work
Character Comparison
Oral Tradition

Objective: Weighing the traits of Greek and Norse characters.
Enacting oral tradition through a revision and continuation of a myth.

Activity I

The tragic story of Signy shares similar traits with the story of Clytemnestra, as told in chapter seventeen. Complete the comparison chart in order to attain a better understanding of the similarities and differences between the two women.

Comparison Chart

Question	Clytemnestra	Signy
What is the motive for revenge?		
Who is the target of revenge?		
How long did she wait to be avenged?		
Did she have an accomplice? If so, who?		
Is the revenge satisfying?		
How did she die?		
Do you think her revenge was justified or unjustified?		
How does she depict the women of her culture (Greek and Norse)?		

Activity II

Create a myth of your own using any combination of the following:

- two heroes or heroines
- one or two gods or goddesses
- a difficult task
- an act of vengeance
- a solution that involves a payback
- a friendship or love involving people and gods or goddesses
- the intervention of a god or goddess
- a death
- a rebirth as something else

Activity II

Create a myth of your own using any combination of the following:

- two heroes or heroines
- one or two gods or goddesses
- a difficult task
- an act of vengeance
- a solution that involves a payback
- a friendship or love involving people and gods or goddesses
- the intervention of a god or goddess
- a death
- a rebirth as something else

Chapter 23
Reading for Details
Critical Thinking

Objective: Comparing the Greek and Norse gods.

Activity I

Several Greek and Norse gods share similar traits and responsibilities. In the following comparison chart, write the Greek god who most accurately resembles the Norse god.

Comparison Chart

	Norse god	Greek god
1.	Odin	*Zeus*
2.	Frigga	*Hera*
3.	Hela	*Persephone*
4.	Tyr	*Ares*
5.	Freya	*Aphrodite*
6.	Thor	*Zeus / Athena*

Activity II

In the *Book of Genesis,* the serpent convinces Eve to eat forbidden fruit. As a result, God punishes mankind. The serpent also has an evil image in Norse mythology. Hamilton writes:

> "Over Yggdrasil, as over Asgard, hung the threat of destruction. Like the gods it was doomed to die. A serpent and his brood gnawed continually at the root beside Niflheim, Hel's home. Some day they would succeed in killing the tree, and the universe would come crashing down." (Pg. 327)

Notice the similar representation of the serpent between the two cultures. Write a brief paragraph giving your opinion of why the serpent commonly symbolizes evil and treachery through the ages.

Answers will vary.
One theory is that mankind has certain common symbols of association, such as the snake for evil, that are carried through centuries and civilizations.

Chapter 23
Reading for Details
Critical Thinking

Objective: Comparing the Greek and Norse gods.

Activity I

Several Greek and Norse gods share similar traits and responsibilities. In the following comparison chart, write the Greek god who most accurately resembles the Norse god.

Comparison Chart

Norse god	Greek god
1. Odin	
2. Frigga	
3. Hela	
4. Tyr	
5. Freya	
6. Thor	

Activity II

In the *Book of Genesis,* the serpent convinces Eve to eat forbidden fruit. As a result, God punishes mankind. The serpent also has an evil image in Norse mythology. Hamilton writes:

> "Over Yggdrasil, as over Asgard, hung the threat of destruction. Like the gods it was doomed to die. A serpent and his brood gnawed continually at the root beside Niflheim, Hel's home. Some day they would succeed in killing the tree, and the universe would come crashing down." (Pg. 327)

Notice the similar representation of the serpent between the two cultures. Write a brief paragraph giving your opinion of why the serpent commonly symbolizes evil and treachery through the ages.

Chapters 22-23
Reading for Details

Objective: Gaining insight into the morals and customs of the Germanic people.

Activity I

The historian Cornelius Tacitus (55-116 C.E.) acted as a traveling administrator for outlying regions of the Roman Empire at the time of its greatest expansion. In his work *On the Origin, Geography, Institutions and Tribes of the Germans* (*Germania*), Tacitus compares the virtues and vigor of the semi-civilized Germanic peoples to what he viewed as a deteriorating Roman society. Read the following excerpt from his work and answer the questions that follow.

       They choose their kings for their noble birth, their commanders for their valour. The power even of the kings is not absolute or arbitrary. The commanders rely on example rather than on the authority of their rank—on the admiration they win by showing conspicuous energy and courage and by pressing forward in front of their own troops. Capitol punishment, imprisonment, even flogging, are allowed to none but the priests, and are not inflicted merely as punishments or on the commanders' orders, but as it were in obedience to the god whom the Germans believe to be present on the fields of battle. They actually carry with them into the fight certain figures and emblems taken from their sacred groves. A specially powerful incitement to valour is that the squadrons and divisions are not made up at random by the mustering of chance-comers, but are each composed of men of one family or clan. Close by them, too, are their nearest and dearest, so that they can hear the shrieks of their womenfolk and the wailing of their children. These are the witnesses whom each man reverences most highly, whose praise he most desires. It is to their mothers and wives that they go to have their wounds treated, and the women are not afraid to count and compare the gashes. They also carry supplies of food to the combatants and encourage them.
       It stands on record that armies already wavering and on the point of collapse have been rallied by the women, pleading heroically with their men, thrusting forward their bared bosoms, and making them realize the imminent prospect of enslavement—a fate which the Germans fear more desperately for their women than for themselves. Indeed, you can secure a surer hold on these nations if you compel them to include among a consignment of hostages some girls of noble family. More than this, they believe that there resides in women an element of holiness and a gift of prophecy; and so they do not scorn to ask their advice, or lightly disregard their replies....

Chapters 22-23
Reading for Details

Objective: Gaining insight into the morals and customs of the Germanic people.

Activity I

The historian Cornelius Tacitus (55-116 C.E.) acted as a traveling administrator for outlying regions of the Roman Empire at the time of its greatest expansion. In his work *On the Origin, Geography, Institutions and Tribes of the Germans* (*Germania*), Tacitus compares the virtues and vigor of the semi-civilized Germanic peoples to what he viewed as a deteriorating Roman society. Read the following excerpt from his work and answer the questions that follow.

They choose their kings for their noble birth, their commanders for their valour. The power even of the kings is not absolute or arbitrary. The commanders rely on example rather than on the authority of their rank—on the admiration they win by showing conspicuous energy and courage and by pressing forward in front of their own troops. Capitol punishment, imprisonment, even flogging, are allowed to none but the priests, and are not inflicted merely as punishments or on the commanders' orders, but as it were in obedience to the god whom the Germans believe to be present on the fields of battle. They actually carry with them into the fight certain figures and emblems taken from their sacred groves. A specially powerful incitement to valour is that the squadrons and divisions are not made up at random by the mustering of chance-comers, but are each composed of men of one family or clan. Close by them, too, are their nearest and dearest, so that they can hear the shrieks of their womenfolk and the wailing of their children. These are the witnesses whom each man reverences most highly, whose praise he most desires. It is to their mothers and wives that they go to have their wounds treated, and the women are not afraid to count and compare the gashes. They also carry supplies of food to the combatants and encourage them.

It stands on record that armies already wavering and on the point of collapse have been rallied by the women, pleading heroically with their men, thrusting forward their bared bosoms, and making them realize the imminent prospect of enslavement—a fate which the Germans fear more desperately for their women than for themselves. Indeed, you can secure a surer hold on these nations if you compel them to include among a consignment of hostages some girls of noble family. More than this, they believe that there resides in women an element of holiness and a gift of prophecy; and so they do not scorn to ask their advice, or lightly disregard their replies....

On matters of minor importance only the chiefs debate; on major affairs, the whole community. But even where the commons have the decision, the subject is considered in advance by the chiefs. Except in case of accident or emergency, they assemble on certain particular days, either shortly after the new moon or shortly before the full moon. These, they hold, are the most auspicious times for embarking on any enterprise. They do not reckon time by days, as we do, but by nights. All their engagements and appointments are made on this system. Night is regarded as ushering in the day. It is a drawback of their independent spirit that they do not take a summons as a command: instead of coming to a meeting all together, they waste two or three days by their unpunctuality. When the assembled crowd thinks fit, they take their seats fully armed. Silence is then commanded by the priests, who on such occasions have power to enforce obedience. Then such hearing is given to the king or state-chief as his age, rank, military distinction, or eloquence can secure—more because his advice carries weight than because he has the power to command....

The Assembly is competent also to bear criminal charges, especially those involving the risk of capitol punishment. The mode of execution varies according to the offense. These same assemblies elect, among other officials, the magistrates who administer justice in the districts and villages....

Their marriage code is strict, and no feature of their morality deserves higher praise. They are almost unique among barbarians in being content with one wife apiece—all of them, that is, except a very few who take more than one wife not to satisfy their desires but because their exalted rank brings them many pressing offers of matrimonial alliances. The dowry is brought by husband to wife, not by wife to husband. Parents and kinsmen attend and approve the gifts—not gifts chosen to please a woman's fancy or gaily deck a young bride, but oxen, a horse with its bridle, or a shield, spear, and sword. In consideration of such gifts a man gets his wife, and she in her turn brings a present of arms to her husband. The inter-change of gifts typifies for them the most sacred bond of union, sanctified by mystic rites under the favour of the presiding deities of wedlock. That is why she is reminded, in the very ceremonies which bless her marriage at its outset, that she enters her husband's home to be the partner of his toils and perils, that both in peace and in war she is to share his sufferings and adventures. On these terms she must live her life and bear her children....

On matters of minor importance only the chiefs debate; on major affairs, the whole community. But even where the commons have the decision, the subject is considered in advance by the chiefs. Except in case of accident or emergency, they assemble on certain particular days, either shortly after the new moon or shortly before the full moon. These, they hold, are the most auspicious times for embarking on any enterprise. They do not reckon time by days, as we do, but by nights. All their engagements and appointments are made on this system. Night is regarded as ushering in the day. It is a drawback of their independent spirit that they do not take a summons as a command: instead of coming to a meeting all together, they waste two or three days by their unpunctuality. When the assembled crowd thinks fit, they take their seats fully armed. Silence is then commanded by the priests, who on such occasions have power to enforce obedience. Then such hearing is given to the king or state-chief as his age, rank, military distinction, or eloquence can secure—more because his advice carries weight than because he has the power to command....

The Assembly is competent also to bear criminal charges, especially those involving the risk of capitol punishment. The mode of execution varies according to the offense. These same assemblies elect, among other officials, the magistrates who administer justice in the districts and villages....

Their marriage code is strict, and no feature of their morality deserves higher praise. They are almost unique among barbarians in being content with one wife apiece—all of them, that is, except a very few who take more than one wife not to satisfy their desires but because their exalted rank brings them many pressing offers of matrimonial alliances. The dowry is brought by husband to wife, not by wife to husband. Parents and kinsmen attend and approve the gifts—not gifts chosen to please a woman's fancy or gaily deck a young bride, but oxen, a horse with its bridle, or a shield, spear, and sword. In consideration of such gifts a man gets his wife, and she in her turn brings a present of arms to her husband. The inter-change of gifts typifies for them the most sacred bond of union, sanctified by mystic rites under the favour of the presiding deities of wedlock. That is why she is reminded, in the very ceremonies which bless her marriage at its outset, that she enters her husband's home to be the partner of his toils and perils, that both in peace and in war she is to share his sufferings and adventures. On these terms she must live her life and bear her children....

Questions:

1.   What value did German society seem to place on women? What might be surmised about gender relationships in Germanic society?

   Women were valued for their nursing skills, encouragement, and as a source of advice. Women were also believed to have an element of holiness and to possess prophetic gifts.

2.   What are the governmental and/or judicial functions of the kings? The priests? The Assembly?

   Kings control meetings of the chiefs and the community when they gather to discuss affairs of the people. The priests control the peace at these gatherings. The Assembly executes criminal charges and elects magistrates.

3.   On what particular virtues of the Germanic societies does Tacitus seem to lay the greatest stress?

   Tacitus lays the highest praise upon their strict marriage code.

4.   What is the woman reminded of in the marriage ceremonies?

   The woman knows she is a partner with her husband and will endure all of his toils and perils. She will share his sufferings and adventures.

Questions:

1.   What value did German society seem to place on women? What might be surmised about gender relationships in Germanic society?

2.   What are the governmental and/or judicial functions of the kings? The priests? The Assembly?

3.   On what particular virtues of the Germanic societies does Tacitus seem to lay the greatest stress?

4.   What is the woman reminded of in the marriage ceremonies?

Wrap-Up

The night sky is a group of images from a number of different societies, both ancient and modern. Most ancient cultures saw pictures in the stars of the night sky, and the earliest known efforts to catalogue the stars date to cuneiform texts and artifacts roughly 6000 years old. When you check your horoscope, you are following an age-old tradition of reading the planets for predictions of the future. Your horoscope is based upon the position of the stars and planets in relation to one another at the hour of your birth. The zodiac, consisting of twelve constellations, is the basis for the horoscope.

1. The ancient Greeks have by far contributed the most towards explanations for the Zodiac signs. In the following chart, match the proper myth to its corresponding zodiacal constellation. You may need to use an encyclopedia or the Internet to obtain all the answers.

Zodiac Sign	**Mythological Explanation**
Aquarius _____	A. The crab sent to harass Hercules
Aries _____	B. The archer Chiron; substitute for Prometheus
Cancer _____	C. The water carrier Ganymede; cupbearer for gods
Gemini _____	D. The virgin Astraea; spirit of justice for men
Leo _____	E. The scorpion responsible for Orion's death
Libra _____	F. The ram of the Golden Fleece sought by Jason
Pisces _____	G. The Sea Goat; form Bacchus takes on to rescue Jupiter from the giant Typhoeus
Sagittarius _____	H. The bull-form Jupiter takes on to kidnap Europa
Scorpio _____	I. Twin brothers Castor and Pollux; adventurers
Taurus _____	J. The fish; form Venus and Cupid take on to escape the giant Typhoeus
Virgo _____	K. The Nemean lion; killed by Hercules
Capricorn _____	L. The scales; the balance of the universe

Answer Key:
1. C	5. K	9. E
2. F	6. L	10. H
3. A	7. J	11. D
4. I	8. B	12. G

2. Design a new constellation and draw a picture of it.. Create and write a myth

Wrap-Up

The night sky is a group of images from a number of different societies, both ancient and modern. Most ancient cultures saw pictures in the stars of the night sky, and the earliest known efforts to catalogue the stars date to cuneiform texts and artifacts roughly 6000 years old. When you check your horoscope, you are following an age-old tradition of reading the planets for predictions of the future. Your horoscope is based upon the position of the stars and planets in relation to one another at the hour of your birth. The zodiac, consisting of twelve constellations, is the basis for the horoscope.

1. The ancient Greeks have by far contributed the most towards explanations for the Zodiac signs. In the following chart, match the proper myth to its corresponding zodiacal constellation. You may need to use an encyclopedia or the Internet to obtain all the answers.

Zodiac Sign		**Mythological Explanation**
Aquarius	_____	A. The crab sent to harass Hercules
Aries	_____	B. The archer Chiron; substitute for Prometheus
Cancer	_____	C. The water carrier Ganymede; cupbearer for gods
Gemini	_____	D. The virgin Astraea; spirit of justice for men
Leo	_____	E. The scorpion responsible for Orion's death
Libra	_____	F. The ram of the Golden Fleece sought by Jason
Pisces	_____	G. The Sea Goat; form Bacchus takes on to rescue Jupiter from the giant Typhoeus
Sagittarius	_____	
Scorpio	_____	H. The bull-form Jupiter takes on to kidnap Europa
Taurus	_____	I. Twin brothers Castor and Pollux; adventurers
Virgo	_____	J. The fish; form Venus and Cupid take on to escape the giant Typhoeus
Capricorn	_____	
		K. The Nemean lion; killed by Hercules
		L. The scales; the balance of the universe

2. Design a new constellation and draw a picture of it.. Create and write a myth

Appendix I

SMALL GROUP LEARNING

Small Group Learning is defined as two to five students working together for a common goal. For it to be successful, three basic elements must be present.

1. **SOCIAL SKILLS IN GROUP WORK:** Most students, unless they are taught the appropriate skills, do not participate as effectively as they might in small group work. Like any other skill, those needed for group work must be identified, practiced, and reinforced. To this end, we have included a Social Skills Behavior Checklist which we will ask you to use to rate your group. At this time, please read the related objectives listed below.

Social-Behavioral Objectives
1. Everyone is addressed by his or her first name.
2. Everyone speaks quietly in order not to disturb other groups.
3. No one ever uses put-downs or name calling.
4. Everyone is always physically and mentally part of the group. The following are prohibited and may result in the group's grade being lowered:
    A. Putting one's head down on the desk.
    B. Reading or working on unrelated items.
    C. Moving about the room or talking to members of other groups.
5. Everyone is encouraged to participate and does participate.
6. Everyone offers praise and encouragement.
7. Everyone recognizes that on some points of opinion two equally valid points of view can be supported.
8. Everyone also recognizes, however, that the worth of an idea (opinion) depends on the strength of the facts that support it.

Social-Intellectual Objectives
9. Ideas are discussed aloud.
10. Ideas are summarized.
11. Clarification is asked for and received.
12. Explanations are given until everyone understands.
13. Ideas, not people, are criticized.
14. Difficult ideas are paraphrased.
15. Multiple points of view are examined.
16. Work is organized within available time and available resources.
17. Questions are asked and answered satisfactorily.
18. Ideas are examined, elaborated on, and pulled together.
19. Reasons and rationale are asked for and provided.
20. Conclusions are challenged with new information.
21. Ideas are created in brainstorming.

2.   **POSITIVE INTERDEPENDENCE:** Critical to successful *group work* is the realization on the part of the students "that we are all in this together; we either sink or swim as a group." In terms of this unit, it may mean that everyone in the group will share the group grade on the project, whether it is an "A" or an "F."

3.   **INDIVIDUAL ACCOUNTABILITY:** The bottom line of any teaching method is, of course, how well the students have mastered the objectives being taught. Therefore, you must understand that the small group process, while it is more fun than other methods, is serious business. At the conclusion of this unit, a test may be used to evaluate how well each individual has mastered the objectives. As a consequence, the student who slacks off in the group or in his homework not only lets the group down, but also hurts him or herself.

PROCEDURES FOR SMALL GROUP WORK

As well as mastery of content and concepts, grades will be based on the demonstration of the following skills.

1. **Linguistic-Intellectual Skills** – These skills are fostered when students examine ideas from multiple points of view and critically probe for strengths and weaknesses.
2. **Group Social Skills** – Before anything else can be mastered, the small group must function effectively as a learning unit, which makes the mastery of these skills the first priority.

Linguistic-Intellectual Skills to be Demonstrated	Examples of these skills in action
Explaining	It seems to me… One way of looking at it… How does everyone feel about… The idea that…
Encouraging	What's your idea? I didn't think of that. Good idea! That helps. Good; go on with that thought.
Clarifying Let's put it this way...	Perhaps if we draw a chart... It may mean that.... How does this sound... Where does this lead us?
Elaborating	That's right and it also may include... Another instance of that is when... A point we might also include...
Qualifying	I agree with your premise, but... I see it leading somewhere else... That is one reason, but it may also... I agree with the examples, but I come to a different conclusion. Does that conclusion hold up in every instance?
Questioning	Why do you say that? What is the proof for that conclusion? Is that a valid generalization? How did you reach that point?
Disagreeing	It seems to me there could be a different reason. But looking at it from his point of view... We may be jumping to a conclusion without looking at all the facts. Here's another way of looking at it...

A-3

SMALL GROUP EVALUATION SHEET

Social-Behavioral Skills in our group	Poor			Good	
1. Everyone is addressed by his or her first name.	1	2	3	4	5
2. Everyone speaks quietly. (If one group gets loud, other groups get louder to hear each other.)	1	2	3	4	5
3. No one ever uses put-downs or name calling.	1	2	3	4	5
4. Everyone is always physically and mentally part of the group.	1	2	3	4	5
5. Everyone is encouraged to and does participate.	1	2	3	4	5
6. Everyone offers praise and encouragement.	1	2	3	4	5
7. Everyone recognizes that on some opinions, two equally valid points of view can be supported.	1	2	3	4	5
8. Everyone also recognizes, however, that the worth of an idea (opinion) depends on the strength of the facts that support it.	1	2	3	4	5

Social-Intellectual Skills in our group

	Poor			Good	
9. Ideas are examined and discussed aloud.	1	2	3	4	5
10. Ideas are summarized.	1	2	3	4	5
11. Clarification is asked for and received.	1	2	3	4	5
12. Explanations are given until everyone understands.	1	2	3	4	5
13. Ideas, not people, are criticized.	1	2	3	4	5
14. Difficult ideas are paraphrased.	1	2	3	4	5
15. Multiple points of view are examined.	1	2	3	4	5
16. Work is organized within available time and available resources.	1	2	3	4	5
17. Questions are asked and answered satisfactorily.	1	2	3	4	5
18. Ideas are examined, elaborated on, and pulled together.	1	2	3	4	5
19. Reasons and rationales are asked for and provided.	1	2	3	4	5
20. Conclusions are challenged with new information.	1	2	3	4	5
21. Ideas are created in brainstorming.	1	2	3	4	5

Total Score _____

STUDENT ROLES IN GROUP DISCUSSIONS

1. **Reader:** The reader's job is to read the questions aloud and to be sure everyone knows the meaning of unfamiliar words and understands the questions.

2. **Recorder:** The recorder takes notes and is responsible for writing down the group's final answers.

3. **Timer and Voice Monitor:** The timer and voice monitor is responsible for reminding individuals when they get too loud and for keeping track of the time. Because of a concern for finishing the project on time, the monitor will be the one to get the students back on task when they stray or get bogged down on one point.

4. **Checker and Encourager:** This person's chief responsibility is to encourage all members to contribute, to compliment when appropriate, and to remind everyone of the necessity of avoiding name calling and/or put-downs.

Appendix II

Newspaper

News Article - This is an accurate and objective reporting of an event. News articles should include the "Five W's": What, When, Where, Who, and Why. A good newspaper writer usually can include all the necessary information in the first paragraph of the article. This is done so that readers can understand what the article is about simply by reading one paragraph and then deciding if they want to read further to get more detailed information.

The next paragraphs in the news article expand on the Five W's of the first paragraph.

Example:
Last night at 10 PM, a train from Philadelphia, PA to Pittsburgh slid off the tracks near Johnstown. No injuries were reported, but the train had been carrying flammable materials. A spokesperson for the Pennsylvania Railroad, Mr. Robert Graves, said that while there was no evidence of sabotage, "that possibility is being looked into police." This is the second derailing on this route in two years.

The rest of the article would expand upon and give background and further information on the accident.

Editorial - This is a piece in which the writer gives opinions about an issue. A possible solution may be suggested. The requirements of the Five W's and absolute, unbiased accuracy are not adhered to as strictly as they are in a news article.

Example:
How many train wrecks will we have before the government steps in? Will it take a fatality before trains in our state are made safer? Should explosives, poisonous materials, and hazardous wastes continue to be shipped with only minor considerations to safety? This newspaper's opinion is a firm and resounding "No!" If the Federal Transportation Commission does not recognize its own failings and correct the problems, it will be our local politicians' job to re-route trains carrying potentially dangerous cargoes away from our communities.

Human-Interest Story - This type differs from the previous two because it has a different overall intent. As in a news article, the intent is to inform the reader of facts, but in the human-interest story, writers add the element of appealing to the readers' sympathies. Answering the Five W's is usually adhered to, but not as strictly as in the news article. Frequent topics of human-interest stories are animals, heroic deeds, strange occurrences of fate, money, etc.

Example:
Huddled among the broken railroad cars and destroyed contents of yesterday's train derailment near us, sat someone's lost puppy. Police found it early this morning after hearing whimpering from inside one of the cars. The poor dog's leg had been severed in the accident, and it was trapped by rubble. Had another hour elapsed, it probably would have died, says a local veterinarian, who treated the mixed-breed, black-and-white dog. According to the vet, Stumpy, as the dog is now called, has received more than twenty requests for adoption since his lucky rescue was accomplished.

Headline – This is a short heading over an article, which is set in large type, and which gives an indication of the subject of the article. Headlines are short and are designed to catch the readers' interest. All important words in the headline should be capitalized. Each article in a newspaper contains a headline. The wording of headlines is very important. If they say too much, readers may skip reading the article; if they are too vague, the subject may not interest the reader. Simple words such as *a, and, the* are frequently left out of headlines.

Examples:
Train Jumps Tracks; Second in Two Years

Two Train Wrecks Are Too Many

Injured Puppy Found in Train Debris

Appendix III

Dramatization of Scenes in the Novel

Drama: Drama according to Aristotle is "imitated human action" presented through dialogue meant to instruct or entertain.

Dramatic Monologue: A person speaks to a silent audience, revealing an aspect of his or her character, expressing a viewpoint.

Comments: Often, sections of literary works seem to portray intense or captivating interaction, drama, between characters. While reading, visualize how the characters move in terms of their gestures and in relation to each other. See them touching each other or backing away. Hear the tones in their voices and the inflections, volume, and emphasis they use when they speak to each other. Imaginatively experience the feelings and meanings they are communicating to each other.

We do not expect that students will be above-average performers, and we do not feel they should be judged on "acting" as a major criterion in any dramatization. Students should be expected to capture the characters they portray and exhibit the truth of whatever the activity calls for. These types of activities are not intended to be polished Hollywood performances, nor the quality one would even see on a High School stage. That takes a class in drama or a group of talented performers who have a great deal of time to prepare. Our acting activities are designed only to reveal character or plot to the audience.

Appendix IV

Directions for Interviews

Planning in Small Groups

First, discuss what you, as interviewer, want to know and the reasons you want to know it. Decide what you want to use as your specific questions.

Second, anticipate what the person being interviewed will answer. Use as many quotations from the text as possible. The answers should be consistent with things the character or narrative text says.

Finally, plan the interviewer's summary remark. Try to explain how the information in the questions/answers relates to the plot in general and thematic ideas of the novel.

Mythology

Terms and Definitions

Anecdote - A brief story that is usually illustrative or humorous; similar to a vignette.

Characterization - the methods, incidents, speech, etc., an author uses to reveal the people in the book.

Climax - the point of greatest dramatic tension or excitement in a story. Example: Othello's murder of Desdemona.

Deus ex Machina - the intervention into the plot of a person, force, or unexpected occurrence which resolves a seemingly impossible situation. Example: A forest is about to be destroyed, along with the hero, by a fire, but a drenching rain suddenly puts out the blaze.

Dialogue - conversation between two or more characters.

Epic - a long, narrative poem which celebrates the deeds of legendary heroes. Example: *The Iliad.*

Epic Hero - a man (very rarely a woman) who seems to conquer most problems he encounters, and who is usually protected by or descended from gods but does not possess any god-like powers himself. He is faithful to family, country, and the gods. He is brave, tries to overcome evil with good, is intelligent, and is guided by the gods. Because they feel fear and make mistakes, epic heroes are not supermen; however, their faults do not hinder their ability to overcome their trials and tribulations. In the case of *The Odyssey*, the epic hero Odysseus is also able to talk his way out of many situations through fabricated stories. He is creative in his problem solving and a practiced diplomat.

Epithets - an adjective or phrase which delineates a personality by the attributes possessed by the person or thing. These epithets help the reader understand the characters' important characteristics. Example: Achilles the invincible.

The Homeric epithet is a phrase, usually a compound adjective, which is used frequently to describe a thing or person. Examples:
• "rosy-fingered Dawn"
• "the wine-dark sea."

Hero - the central character, usually one who possesses noble qualities such as self-sacrifice, courage, wisdom, etc. Examples: Tarzan, Frodo, Jesus.

Imagery - the use of words to evoke sensory impressions that are beyond the words themselves. Similar to *symbol* and *motif.* Example: "Get thee to a nunnery," from *Hamlet* implies purity and chastity, not simply a convent.

Inference - the act of drawing a conclusion that is not actually stated. For example, in *The Pigman,* since John and Lorraine are writing a memorial epic about the incident with the Pigman, we may infer that the Pigman is now dead and the incident is important to them.

Irony - a subtle, sometimes humorous perception of inconsistency in which the significance of a statement or event is changed by its content. For example: the firehouse burned down.
- *Dramatic irony* - the audience knows more about a character's situation than the character does, foreseeing an outcome contrary from the character's expectations. The character's statements have one meaning for the character and a different meaning for the reader, who knows more than the character.
- *Structural irony* - a naïve hero whose view of the world differs from the author's and reader's. Structural irony flatters the reader's intelligence at the expense of the hero.
- *Verbal irony* - a discrepancy between what is said and what is really meant; sarcasm. Example: calling a stupid man smart.

Metaphor - a comparison of two things that are basically dissimilar but are brought together in order to create a sharp image. Example: The moon, a haunting lantern, shone through the clouds.

Myth - a story, often told orally, which explains some natural phenomena in imaginative ways. A myth does not have any historical basis, unlike a legend. Myths usually contain supernatural occurrences or characters. Examples: Daedalus and Icarus, primitive creation myths.

Narrator - the one who tells the story. If the narrator is a character in the book, the term is first-person narration. (Example: *Moby Dick* is narrated by Ishmael, a crew member). If the narrator is not a character, the term is third-person narration. (Example: *Sense and Sensibility*).

Oral tradition - the transference of stories, songs, etc., from one generation to another or from one culture to another. Stories told orally are easily forgotten, and it is important that the storyteller frequently remind his listener about important character traits and events.

Oratory - the art of public speaking. A good speech often includes the following elements:
- The speaker talks directly to the audience in a conversational manner, sometimes asking the audience questions and then providing the answers.
- The tone of the speech is often determined by the points the speaker is trying to make. Speeches often have repeated words or phrases included to emphasize ideas and give the speech a pleasing rhythm.
- A speech sometimes contains controversial statements included to deliberately engage the audience's emotions.

Rising Action - the part of the story's plot that adds complications to the problems and increases the reader's interest.

Setting - when and where the short story, play, or novel takes place. Example: *Macbeth* takes place in the eleventh century in Scotland, which greatly influences the story and adds the elements of truthfulness to its violence.

Simile - a comparison between two different things using either *like* or *as*. Example: I am as hungry as a horse.

Symbol - an object, person, or place that has a meaning in itself and that also stands for something larger than itself, usually an idea or concept; some concrete thing which represents an abstraction. Example: The sea could be symbolic for "the unknown;" since the sea is something which is physical and can be seen by the reader, but has elements which cannot be understood, it can be used *symbolically* to stand for the abstraction of "mystery," "obscurity," or "the unknown."

Theme - the central or dominant idea behind the story; the most important aspect that emerges from how the book treats its subject. Sometimes theme is easy to see, but, at other times, it may be more difficult. Theme is usually expressed indirectly, as an element the reader must figure out. It is a universal statement about humanity, rather than a simple statement dealing with plot or characters in the story. Themes are generally hinted at through different devices: a phrase or quotation that introduces the novel, a recurring element in the book, or an observation made that is reinforced through plot, dialogue, or characters. It must be emphasized that not all works of literature have themes in them.
　　In a story about a man who is diagnosed with cancer and, through medicine and will-power, returns to his former occupation, the theme might be: "real courage is demonstrated through internal bravery and perseverance." In a poem about a flower that grows, blooms, and dies, the theme might be: "youth fades and death comes to all."

Tragedy - a serious work, usually a novel, in which the main character experiences defeat. brought about by a tragic flaw. Example: *Hamlet*.

Tragic flaw - the main defect of the protagonist in a tragedy. Example: Hamlet's failure to act causes his death.

The Perfect Balance Between Cost and Quality for Classic Paperbacks

WITH ALL OF THE DIFFERENT EDITIONS of classics available, what makes *Prestwick House Literary Touchstone Classics*™ better?

Our editions were designed by former teachers with the needs of teachers and students in mind. Because we've struggled to stretch tight budgets and had to deal with the deficiencies of cheaply made paperbacks, we've produced high-quality trade editions at remarkably low prices. As a result, our editions have it all.

Value Pricing – With our extraordinary Educators' Discount, you get these books at **50% or more off the list price.**

Reading Pointers for Sharper Insights – Concise notes that encourage students to question and consider points of plot, theme, characterization, and style, etc.

Glossary and Vocabulary – An A-to-Z glossary makes sure that your students won't get lost in difficult allusions or archaic vocabulary and concepts.

Sturdy Bindings and High-Quality Paper – High-quality construction ensures these editions hold up to heavy, repeated use.

Strategies for Understanding Shakespeare – Each *Shakespeare Literary Touchstone Classic*™ contains line numbers, margin notes, and a guide to understanding Shakespeare's language, as well as key strategies for getting the most from the plays.

Special Introductory Discount for Educator's only — At Least 50% Off!

New titles are constantly being added, call or visit our website for current listing.

		Retail Price	Intro. Discount
200053	Adventures of Huckleberry Finn - *Twain* TU RJ AT AP	$4.99	$2.49
200473	Adventures of Tom Sawyer, The - *Twain* TU RJ AT	$4.99	$2.49
202116	Alice's Adventure in Wonderland - *Carroll* TU RJ	$3.99	$1.99
202118	Antigone - *Sophocles* TU RJ AT	$3.99	$1.99
200141	Awakening, The - *Chopin* TU RJ AT AP	$3.99	$1.99
202111	Beowulf - *Roberts (ed.)* TU	$3.99	$1.99
204866	Best of Poe, The: The Tell-Tale Heart, The Raven, The Cask of Amontillado, and 30 Others - *Poe*	$4.99	$2.49
200150	Call of the Wild, The - *London* TU RJ AT	$3.99	$1.99
200348	Canterbury Tales - *Chaucer* TU	$3.99	$1.99
200179	Christmas Carol, A - *Dickens* TU RJ AT	$3.99	$1.99
201198	Crime and Punishment - *Dostoyevsky* TU	$6.99	$3.49
200694	Doll's House, A - *Ibsen* TU RJ AT	$3.99	$1.99
200190	Dr. Jekyll and Mr. Hyde - *Stevenson* TU RJ AT	$3.99	$1.99

202113	Dracula - *Stoker* TU RJ	$5.99
200166	Ethan Frome - *Wharton* TU RJ	$3.99
200054	Frankenstein - *Shelley* TU RJ AT AP	$4.99
202112	Great Expectations - *Dickens* TU RJ AT AP	$5.99
202108	Gulliver's Travels - *Swift* TU	$4.99
200091	Hamlet - *Shakespeare* TU RJ AT AP	$3.99
200074	Heart of Darkness - *Conrad* TU RJ	$3.99
202117	Hound of the Baskervilles, The - *Doyle* TU RJ AT	$3.99
200147	Importance of Being Earnest, The - *Wilde* TU RJ AT	$3.99
301414	Invisible Man, The - *Wells* TU RJ	$3.99
202115	Jane Eyre - *Brontë* TU RJ	$6.99
200146	Julius Caesar - *Shakespeare* TU RJ AT	$3.99
201817	Jungle, The - *Sinclair* TU RJ AT	$5.99
200125	Macbeth - *Shakespeare* TU RJ AT AP	$3.99
204864	Medea - *Euripides* TU	$3.99
200133	Metamorphosis, The - *Kafka* TU RJ	$3.99
200081	Midsummer Night's Dream, A - *Shakespeare* TU RJ AT	$3.99
202123	Much Ado About Nothing - *Shakespeare* TU RJ	$3.99
301391	My Antonia - *Cather* TU RJ	$3.99
200079	Narrative of the Life of Frederick Douglass - *Douglass* TU RJ AT	$3.99
301269	Odyssey, The - *Butler (trans.)* TU RJ AT	$4.99
200564	Oedipus Rex - *Sophocles* TU	$3.99
200095	Othello - *Shakespeare* TU RJ AT AP	$3.99
202121	Picture of Dorian Gray, The - *Wilde* TU RJ	$4.99
200368	Pride and Prejudice - *Austen* TU RJ AT	$4.99
202114	Prince, The - *Machiavelli* TU	$3.99
200791	Pygmalion - *Shaw* TU	$3.99
200102	Red Badge of Courage, The - *Crane* TU RJ AT	$3.99
200193	Romeo and Juliet - *Shakespeare* TU RJ AT	$3.99
200132	Scarlet Letter, The - *Hawthorne* TU AT AP	$4.99
202119	Siddhartha - *Hesse* TU RJ AT	$3.99
204863	Silas Marner - *Eliot* TU RJ AT	$3.99
200251	Tale of Two Cities, A - *Dickens* AT AP	$5.99
200231	Taming of the Shrew, The - *Shakespeare* TU RJ AT	$3.99
204865	Time Machine, The - *Wells* TU RJ AT	$3.99
202120	Treasure Island - *Stevenson* TU RJ	$4.99
301420	War of the Worlds - *Wells* TU RJ	$3.99
202122	Wuthering Heights - *Brontë* TU AT	$5.99

TU **Teaching Units**   RJ **Response Journals**   AT **Activity Pack**   AP **AP Teaching Units**

PH PRESTWICK HOUSE, INC.
"Everything for the English Classroom!"

P.O. Box 658 • Clayton, DE 19938 • (800) 932-4593 • (888) 718-9333 • www.prestwickhouse.com

PRESTWICK HOUSE, INC.

Order Form

Call 1-800-932-4593 Fax 1-888-718-9333

Prestwick House, Inc.
P.O. Box 658
Clayton, DE 19938

Bill To: ■Home ■School

School:

Name:

Address:

City, State, Zip:

Phone: Email:

Ship To: ■Home ■School

School:

Name:

Address:

City, State, Zip:

Phone: Email:

ITEM NO	TITLE	QUANTITY	X	PRICE	=	TOTAL

Subtotal $

Shipping
12% S&H ($6.00 minimum) $

Total $

Method of Payment (Choose one)

❏ **Check or Money Order Enclosed**

❏ Visa ❏ MasterCard ❏ Discover Card ❏ American Express

Signature

Telephone #   Exp. Date

Credit Card #

❏ **Purchase Order Enclosed**
We accept purchase orders and authorized orders charged to institutions. Personal orders not on a credit card must be accompanied by a check.

Shipping & Handling
For orders of $50.00 or less, please add $6.00 for shipping and handling charges. For orders from $50.01 to $799.99 add 12% For orders of $800.00 and more, add 10%

Delivery Service
Most orders are shipped FedEx and you can expect delivery within 7-10 working days. Items in stock are usually shipped within one working day of receiving your order.

Expedited Delivery
for expedited delivery ask about the following options:
• Overnight Air
• 2nd day air
• 3 Day Select